97 Causes for Failure

Ahmed Ragab Ali Abdelghany and Msytr

Published by Msytr, 2024.

97 CAUSES FOR FAILURE

First edition. November 29, 2024.

ISBN: 979-8230538561

Written by Ahmed Ragab Ali Abdelghany and Msytr.

Table of Contents

Table of Contents

✓ Chapter One/ Identity

The chapter discusses the causes of failure related to your personal and corporate identity, what you want, and what your plan is to implement what you desire. It also discusses twelve reasons for failure in this aspect, starting with not knowing who you are or what your organization is. It ends with the haste of results, passing through unchosen role models, the illusion of success, distraction, competition, involvement, group identity, and arrogance in advice or accepting it, and blind imitation...

✓ Chapter Two/ The Environment

This chapter discusses the reasons for failure related to the environment, and perhaps I did not delve into it further because I am firmly convinced that successful institutions and individuals can do so even in corrupt environments despite the difficulties. But let's say that these reasons include a demoralizing environment, ranging from corruption to social corruption, through randomness and favoritism, lack of resources, collective monopoly, and the inability to accept unjustified interference in privacy.

Perhaps many reasons for failure related to the environment, but I focused on the most important reasons that are difficult to overcome and should be avoided, while others can be overcome by humans, and sometimes even benefit from them...

✓ Chapter Three / Habits

This chapter discusses the ten most common habits that cause failure, as these habits are considered, in themselves, reasons that hinder success. They start with closing your ears or talking more than listening and reading, and end with excessive complaining and criticism, through reliance on memory in planning and the offensive tongue, rapid anger, rapid conclusion, and impatience, and waking up late without a reason, and routine, and optimism or pessimism or emotionalism in expectations. It discusses situations in each of them and how this reason prevents you from achieving your desires.

✓ **Chapter Four/Priorities**

This chapter may be shorter because it is basically discussing one reason for failure, which is the lack of determination or inability to determine the priorities in your life and which affects more than the other because you may find that there is a conflict between two things when you make a decision between two or more reasons. I underestimated this and so you had to understand which priority

✓ **Chapter Five/Steps**

This chapter discusses the reasons that lead you to failure and associated with the steps in implementing your project, intending, or intending to the company, if you are talking about an institution, including ten reasons, starting to implement before planning to the absence of evaluation and taking opinions from the beneficiaries or evaluating the peers and passing through the absence of the plan from the basis or importing the prepared plans In advance, not to write down the plans, the margin of plans and the wrong measures of the extent of progress, the lack of realism of the plans, the stagnation of plans, and the absence of the timeless time sometimes

✓ **Chapter Six / Principles**

This chapter discusses the reasons that lead you to failure and are related to principles. Whether you mean failure personally or institutionally, it is impossible to forget the aspect of deviation from the fundamental principles. We will discuss these ten reasons starting with the absence of principles, through their lack of clarity and legitimacy, forgetting them, giving up those principles under the provisions of the gradient and the one-time position, distorting their forms, the absence of reviews for these principles, or rushing into their creation, and the dual standards at times.

✓ **Chapter Seven / Reputation**

This chapter discusses the reasons for failure related to the reputation of the institution or the individual. Here we mention six reasons, including the absence of knowledge initially, a bad reputation, the peacock reputation, exaggerated reputation, trendy reputation, and spectacular failure in reputation.

✓ **Chapter Eight /Opportunities**

This chapter discusses the causes of failure associated with opportunities, and we mention fourteen because

The perspective of crossing the river, adaptation, narrow perspective, perspective of pluralism, criminal conditions, and tasteful quality

✓ **Chapter 9/ Challenges**

This chapter discusses the causes of failure related to challenges and mentions sixteen reasons for it, including ignorance of the challenges, ignoring the challenges, wasting time in complaining, the wrong understanding of challenges and solutions, temporary solutions to challenges, the pessimistic view, inconsistent evaluations, reliability of inaccurate reports, importing solutions, personalizing challenges, the fire-fighting perspective, the perspective of all against all, the cycle of revenge, the perspective of absolute doubt, the perspective of a part of the whole, and the perspective of shipwreck.

✓ **Tenth Chapter / Value**

This chapter discusses the causes of failure related to value and its measurements and considerations, and mentions ten reasons for it, including ignorance of value, market valuation, ignoring the missing value, ignoring the validity of value, poor storage of value, high inflation rates, the benchmark value, the wrong appreciation of value, algebraic calculation of value, and uncalculated values.

Introduction

Introduction

Recently... with the increasing similarity between our brains... and with the increasing imitation and lack of out-of-the-box thinking...

With the confinement of thought to mere rumors or trends... and with the advancement of science until it is counted in the thousands and some deny the others...

With the increasing scientific and non-scientific output available here and there...

It is no longer a matter of resource scarcity as some believe, for resources have become abundant and comfort has become unnoticeable, and now humans are in a maze...

It is not a scarcity maze, but an abundance maze...

It is not a time scarcity problem as claimed, but time is time, and the same 24 hours in a day and night...

But it is a problem of the mind being confined to an idea and science being confined to a maxim, and humans entering the caves of group dancing...

As soon as you enter this place or that institution, you feel that you need to strip your mind of its thoughts and adorn it with those malicious or modern ideas...

And it's just days away, and new ideas are awaiting us..

It makes it obligatory for us to shed the ideas we've worn and put on those more modern ideas on our bodies and in our minds..

This seems to be an epigraph for a book titled "A Nightgown"..

But this won't last long..

I did not accustom this literary style that addresses your feelings, your feeling and forget your thought, mind and doctrine ..

In this book

I wanted to talk to you about a group of the most famous reasons for the failure of people and institutions ... and how these institutions when they fail are the failure of their current managers and the failure of the idea of their primary founders sometimes in creating a continuation of them ..

I also talk to you in this book, a discussion and a participant in understanding the nature of successful works, sustainable projects, and that smart idea that comes out of the mind far away from the act just because others succeeded in this or that his colleague succeeded in that ..

This is a simple sentence you may have heard or read in a book...

We don't have to reinvent the wheel...

Maybe you've heard a friend of mine asking if he can make a program that mimics Telegram...

I asked myself what this nonsense is...

The problem is not that I cannot do it, nor that the project is expensive...

Despite being big problems, the real problem is in the thought and the idea...

How can a person see a successful project and just want to replicate it...

The problem is with that idea that always thinks that copying a successful work will succeed and copying a successful project will succeed...

One day, I was reading a book given to me by a friend... It was titled "Zero to One" or "From Zero to One...

I will discuss some of his ideas with you in advance... But what is striking about this sentence that you won't forget...

Mark Zuckerberg is not going to invent Facebook, and the next Elon Musk is not going to found Tesla...

If Edison had thought in this way, he might have thought of building a large amusement park as one of his projects of his time, or even a night club, or perhaps something that worked for him that he would copy... And not at all to invent an electric lamp...

Perhaps as you see the title, it discusses 97 reasons for failure and not just about the problem of imitation..

But the beginning is always the fundamental foundation and the crucial point in transferring the reader's thought from a conventional person searching for a path to success that others have crossed to that special one who learns from his mistakes and the mistakes of others to create a new path to success that avoids falling into the mistakes of others and also becomes a new path to creating success for himself.

He learns how to hold his pen and perhaps his phone, and he starts with simple scientific thinking that leads him to identify the problem or, rather, to find it and create a project to solve it commercially.

I do not present successful project ideas nor 100 new ideas nor 250 ways to attract customer attention nor 60 ways to convince..

But it is diving into your thoughts and getting to know you and what you want... And what stopped you from reaching and achieving what you want... If you really know what you want...

And here begins the desire to appear in understanding what you want, then think carefully about what others thought and failed at, so you avoid it and plan and work on it... Then you will reach what you want...

When you are convinced that the failed experiences you have had and others have had before you, but because you did not read about the reasons for failure, you repeated them, and you want to succeed despite the fact that others have done so and failed... Isn't that stupid...?

What a fool you are...

When you fall into the same trap repeatedly and you don't realize that others have done this and failed as well.....

And how can you ask for a different result despite repeating the same action in the same circumstances.....?

And how can one say that experience and failure are part of learning

How old is your age to keep trying every mistake that preceded you while people in an era are not content just to understand the mistakes of the past and study and analyze the causes of failure that others have fallen into.. They go on to draw predictive curves deep into the future after the present to learn from mistakes that have not yet occurred and experiences that no one has undertaken and will not undertake..

And you still fear failure... and what matters to you is to succeed.

You don't know perhaps what you want, and you haven't set a measure for success. Perhaps you don't have a plan to achieve it, and perhaps you haven't thought, or thought about why you failed... and why they succeeded... Mat Abbas, the father of Franas, tried to fly as you heard, and I didn't believe it... So should you risk a deadly experiment to succeed?

Or should you analyze the mistake and understand it, and then try again? Perhaps you will fail, but at least you will have taken safety precautions that will make your loss and failure non-lethal...

How can you not fail when you don't know what you want and what your capabilities are...!

When the hardest question for you is what you see yourself doing after five or ten years...

It is not a question about the unknown as some cultures perceive it, but a question about the plan, self-knowledge, and prediction...

So, the causes of tomorrow's wars are already present, and the heroes of tomorrow in sports competitions are now training, and so every future success path has roots and mathematical equations that give you a prediction of its future success...

In this book and throughout its ten chapters

We will explore the reasons for failure together...

And each one will be discussed individually within those chapters, which will divide the reasons into groups of approximately ten reasons with titles...

Perhaps the first is the reason for the idea titled 'Who you are and what you want?'...

Then you will move between the other groups of failure reasons...

And in every chapter, we stop together and remember how many times this reason or those reasons prevented you from achieving your goal, and you didn't realize that it was a cause of failure

The First Chapter

The chapter discusses the causes of failure related to your personal and corporate identity, what you want, and your plan to achieve what you desire. It also discusses twelve causes of failure in this aspect, starting with not knowing who you are or what your organization is. It ends with haste in achieving results, through inappropriate role models, the illusion of success, distraction, competition, involvement, group identity, arrogance in advice or submission to it, emotional thinking, and blind imitation...

I often see this question in job interview questions, and perhaps some ask for a stereotypical answer that they memorize and recite into the listener's ear without realizing the purpose of this question

But it's strange that this question is essential for your life in general and also for your work. If you don't know who you are and what you want, how can you set a plan to implement what you want and how can you move forward...

I'm not here to give you an answer to this question, but to emphasize its importance, understanding, and getting to know yourself better

When you know yourself, perhaps you are a married man with children, which may remind you of your responsibilities. When you know yourself as a civil engineer specializing in smart software or a company manager, you focus on your field of work. When you know yourself as a Muslim or a Christian or a Jew, you look at the aspect of your relationship with God more comprehensively. And when you describe yourself in two lines, you are a man with precision in description

The issue is not just for individuals but also for institutions, organizations, and all other entities. When you don't know the name, vision, message, and goal of the institution, how can you continue to exist? Perhaps one of the reasons for the conflicts within institutions is often the lack of awareness of the vision and message of the institution. Each one of them starts to move towards an idea that deviates from the main goal of the institution. Perhaps they are unaware of the goal, forget it, or maybe it was not set and perhaps it was not agreed upon when joining the institution

The exploration journey that takes place under various names since the first day of new employees within the company to acquaint them with the work environment is not a waste of time, and every time consumed is if in understanding the nature of the human or the company, it prevents the transformation of the human or the employee in the company into something floating without roots, not knowing what it is and what it should do because it does not know what it is and what its institution is that it works with...

Desperately seeking results...

Many of us are looking for the reasons for success and the most effective habits and the way to the moon and how to do it, and focus all their attention on reaching, ignoring what is below it, reminding me of this scene for a person or people carrying a stone on a wooden plank placed on the ground without wheels, and Khalid this young man who advises this person or these people asks them to stop and think carefully to put wheels on this plank so that it can move easier

But focusing on the goal in a way that makes you seek results and cancels out the pause for a moment prevents them from wasting time as they think in assembling the wheels, because from their perspective, it is faster because we will not stop what we are doing and we will keep working hard to move this stone

Perhaps the example is ancient because a person no longer does so after the invention of the wheels, but the present person may do the same in another way when he focuses on the urgency of the results and refuses to waste time thinking and looking at the boundaries of the most far from the situation

How many times do you remember and you open your phone looking for an image and start descending and climbing between thousands of pictures because you did not improve the designation of the image .. And do not know its name or even when you wanted to create a text file and call it a 5 file instead of setting a suitable address for it

The matter may be and you call it a minute or less, but you take every time you search for it for half a minute.

The matter does not stop there, but rather it is away.

Think about this man weighing 200 kilograms who wanted to lose weight. The doctor suggested he eat half a loaf of bread with a little rice at each meal. This man thought that to lose weight faster, he decided to eat only one loaf a day, which meant two meals only...

What will happen? Of course, he will lose his appetite. After two days, he will hate the diet and return to his voracious appetite and eat more than he saved in the previous days...

Desiring quick results . is not only about not thinking about something and planning it, and not only may it turn into intolerance after two days, as with the diet, but it may sometimes lead to opposite results...

Since I have studied nursing, let me point out this example: what if a person taking a medication for a disease decides to stop it to speed up the results? Is it not possible for him to have poisoning instead of the medicine treating him and causing him a disease?

What if you hurried up and said, when I read the table of contents, I will start from the content? Is it not possible that the table of contents contains an introduction that invites you not to finish the book or that you realize that the book is incomplete...

Simply hurrying for results is not contemplating the most important idea in a human's life, which is a journey for him to enjoy, not to reach here or there, but the enjoyment in the journey, my friend...

The unchosen role model...

Perhaps this title is clearer than what has preceded it, for when a human decides to do something, they may emulate those who came before them and learn from them and take lessons from their mistakes or benefit from their experiences...

But what if you make a mistake and instead of emulating a person who did what you want, you emulate another person? I am not saying follow a corrupt person, but at least one who is more different from your culture, thought, and goal. Emulating a football player will not help you become a doctor, and emulating an actor or singer will not make you a successful engineer. Similarly, if your plan is to become a famous wrestler, you do not have to emulate Ahmed Zaki.

When a person chooses a role model, they link their name to success in life. Every time they think about their steps towards achieving their desires, they remember what this role model did and did the same, or were inspired by their thoughts, or even did things not out of necessity just because this role model did them.

But the matter is not only for individuals but also for institutions as well.

What if a university decided to build a new college or a training center or even a university hospital? Is it not necessary for that university, represented by its president or someone acting on his behalf, to go to the best universities instead of the nearest ones geographically?

Is she going to another non-advanced university and asking it to supervise and guide her steps?

The most important matter here is that the role model is not an absolute one, my dear...

What if you thought about learning the card game of cartee

Is he guided by Mustafa Mahmoud or Mustafa Al-Sayed

They are a leader in other sciences

And the matter also applies to institutions

If a university is advanced, it does not necessarily mean it is advanced in all sciences; perhaps if a local university wants to establish a new college in space science, it would have to turn to one of the advanced Russian universities, for example

And although that university is advanced in space science, it is not suitable to be a leader or a role model if the local university wants to establish a special college in nuclear science; perhaps the best option here is an American university

The other matter here is that when you think of a role model for yourself, you must take into account cultural and temporal differences. Perhaps a Hindu enemy's lunch meal will not resemble your lunch meal, and perhaps Napoleon Bonaparte's recreational system in France in past eras may not suit your recreational system...

They are the illusion of success...

I placed this title in this chapter specifically because it results from a misdefinition of yourself or a lack of clarity of the institution's vision...

The illusion of success is a state in which an individual or institution believes that they have achieved what they want without it actually happening, and this is one of the causes of failure. When a person deceives themselves into believing that they have achieved what they want, they may deviate from the path they were on because they no longer have the desire to achieve something. They have already done what they wanted...

Imagine if you had planned to be a doctor or open a business or become a teacher or work for a company

Have you succeeded with this..?

Unfortunately, not

Because you fundamentally knew your point of success wrong

One day I was sitting in one of the cafes

Perhaps my ear caught that sentence wrong

Says one to his companion, What is your income, your salary when you go to propose to a girl... ?

The other, while filling his mouth...... I am a doctor...

Then the other asked him in surprise, "So you're making a lot of money and you're not a doctor...?!!"

Perhaps the salary is not determined by success

But certainly, being a doctor or a teacher or an owner of a factory is not success in itself...

When you decide to be a professional or an expert or an owner of a factory or a shop, your goal is not just to be the owner of something, but those professions and those factories and shops are merely a means to find a continuous source of income to provide a good and enjoyable life and to cover your expenses, perhaps for marriage, perhaps to find a social status, and so on...

Success illusions here may result from a misdefinition of your goal or perhaps incorrect measurements. When you set a goal to earn a certain amount and achieve it by the end of the year, you find that inflation rates have increased and the actual value of the amount is no longer enough to buy what you planned to buy with that amount. Here, you have not succeeded, but rather you have an illusion of success resulting from incorrect measurements...

Remember this person who failed this year and in the end stands in the graduation robe and takes a picture of himself as a success...

Or this man who set a goal to buy a phone...

Then after a while, he sold the TV and bought the phone???...

Success illusion here arises from misdefining the goal, therefore you think you have set the correct scale of success by buying a phone and neglect the fact that you have lost the TV...

So take caution every time you celebrate your success, have you really succeeded in what you want or is it just a success illusion?

Distracted

Distractedness as one of the causes of failure related to your knowledge of yourself and what you want is to do things that do not serve your interests or do not serve your goals or at least less than the other and perhaps thinking about doing more than one thing at the same time...

How many times has your phone rung while you were reading a book and you responded to find a friend calling to joke with you and ask you to go out for dinner or maybe to a bowling alley or even this ad titled "Ten Reasons to Prove Messi is a Fish" on YouTube

How many times have you turned on the TV and sat down to talk to your family and you didn't know if you were talking to them or listening to a play and how many times have you gone out to sit with a friend and sat holding your phone browsing the latest Facebook posts

Neither are you helping anyone nor are you benefiting, or at least your conversation with a friend will benefit you more, and maybe you should end this outing with your friend if it's boring instead of distracting yourself from him with the phone. We thought you were entertained instead of sitting through the boring moment

I put this title in a chapter of not knowing who you are because it is often due to forgetting to answer this question

Who are you and what do you want?

Or what is the institution's vision and what are its goals...

So every time you remember this answer, write it down, review it, and if possible, hang it on the wall, do so...

By doing this, you get rid of sources of distraction not by eliminating the occurrence of distractions, but by ignoring them

Imagine that you called you this stupid person and you did not give him an appointment, then he spoke for half an hour about his plans that he repeats with his bore

What if you asked you for something that is not from your duties, and you looked at your diaries and brought yourself loaded with tasks, so I said to him an excuse I cannot do it or even without excuse

What if you prepared a majestic or weekly time in which yourself retreat and see what you achieved from what you planned ..

This book, which you read now, planned to write it on October 7 of 2023, and here I wrote it in the 2024 of the following year.

If I didn't have a human plan for a joyful friend, a meeting with a colleague, or a new song, I would sit and relax and write it

Unfortunately, you cannot prevent your friend from calling you or your relative who comes without an appointment or this woman who stops you on the street to ask you a long-winded question with trivial details, but you are only able to ignore it and bypass it with a sentence like "I don't have time"

Here, you are not lying, but focusing on your goal and objective, and having a plan, so you don't have time to waste it... Here, with your knowledge of who you are and defining your goals and steps, and setting time frames for them, you don't allow anyone to distract you

We, my dear, in this life, every day, thousands of people look at us as if we are wealth and gains that can be collected. If we do not pay attention, focus, and set our plans, we will not achieve anything.

Competition

It's hard to forget that sentence that success is about escaping from competition from the book "Zero to One "

What if you decided to start a project, went online, searched for successful projects, and said let's imitate one of them

Let's start a printing project on t-shirts and youthful clothing...

Have you thought about how many people do this...

And what is your advantage over them

Maybe this idiot is thinking, what a profitable business! The cost is 3 pounds for each shirt, and I'll get five pounds, and elsewhere they do it for 10 pounds, so I save on it, and people will come to me

But you don't realize that you're competing in something that others can also do

What if he comes third and decides to do the job for four pounds?

And what if the first one decides to offer the service for three and a half pounds or to offer it for free...

You compete and so does everyone else, while you started recently, so your experience is less. Therefore, this person you are competing with may have more experience and be more capable of saving from you.

It's strange that maybe when you offer the service cheaper, you compete on price and forget that you will also be competing with this, and maybe you will be aligned with the idea and live your entire life in competition with others, and maybe your goal will shift from trying to achieve success in providing enough money for your expenses, which you can do in countless ways just because you want to compete with the owner of the store next to you...

Is this really your goal, and have you sat with yourself and reviewed it...?

Do you find this going to the street of the libraries and opening a commercial printing shop, and this opens a market center with a shop to sell vegetables..

It resembles the Egyptian proverb "sells water in the street of water sellers" and continues to compete in services, price, and quality

This is not to say that he does not make a profit, but remember who you are and what you want and what your plan is. You wanted to be a doctor and did not succeed in the high school exam with a score that qualifies you, so you decided to pay a million Egyptian pounds for college fees just because you wanted to be a doctor to compete with this doctor next door. And you forgot that even after you became a doctor, you paid more than him. He made more money and you forgot that you knew your goal wrong and decided to be a doctor with any wish and considered just being a doctor as success..

Then compete and watch your neighbor's wealth increase while you imitate and compete and the cycle continues

This can also happen in institutions as well

Very often, you find that institution moving towards another specialty and neglecting its own just to compete with another company..

Remember, you don't need to compete, my dear. Stop and think and plan. If you come up with a new idea and someone imitates you, there will be progress for you here because you have a vision of what you are doing and previous experience, while the competitor is fully focused on the competition..

Engagement...

What I mean by engagement here as a cause of failure is related to your lack of self-awareness and not knowing what you want to align with the behaviors of the place you are in. You lose your identity and become just this cog in the big factory, working from seven to seven every day, returning to sleep, and repeating the cycle.

The reason why engagement is one of the causes of failure is not because you will not be comfortable in your life, but because over time, you will replace yourself with a cog if you are a worker in a factory under the title of production machinery or replace yourself with just an artificial intelligence tool if you are a web designer or data analyst.

Why is this reason related to self-knowledge?

Because simply replacing your definition of yourself with a sentence like "I am a doctor at hospital S or an engineer in the design department of factory or company P" eliminates your true definition of yourself, and that company will not need you for your entire life, nor will the hospital, even if it does.

But the idea is that sometimes engagement can make you forget what you want from yourself and what your plan is: Can I develop myself? Can I provide additional services? Am I striving for promotion because I offer new ideas or am I striving for promotion just because I do my work correctly?

The first one is a suitable promotion, but if you are doing your work correctly, the alarm in the factory will be better than you, and the artificial intelligence model will not make a mistake, but will do it more accurately, and perhaps after some time it will make suggestions under the name of machine learning and shorten the time and effort required and will not ask for leave.

Therefore, the problem of engagement as a cause of failure is not because you will not rise on the curve of your progress and success, but because even the straight line of your success will not continue.

We are in a developed world where mere preservation of your place is not enough, but you must develop yourself and your capabilities appropriately. The most important thing is to develop, and perhaps the best example of this is that tall building in the nineties by Toyota, as I remember, after a period of time, its height was overshadowed by the surrounding buildings, and it became the shortest in height.

Do not be like that tower, my friend; the other side of engagement is getting involved in the habits around you just because you see them a lot. No, my friend, it is not a reason for you to work in a company where more than one drinks alcohol to do the same.

Remember who you are, what you want, and what steps you need to take to maintain your progress...

Group identity as a cause of failure

Remember this previous example when I told you that the environment where most people drink alcohol is not enough to push you to do so...

The matter cannot simply stop here, and I won't say that I advise them not because the advice is of little value, but because I am confident that most of the advice you will give them has probably been given before. All you are doing by ignoring this environment and leaving it is to possibly devote time to these reasons related to the environment in a dedicated section. But to understand that group identity means that the mistake will be in the waist of everyone in the team; this is the drunkard or the neglectful person in the team when they cause a mistake, you will be one of their victims simply because you are a part of this entity. And as most of the team is bad and indifferent, get rid of being a part of it as soon as possible, without argument and without discussion. But if it is only a minority that commits this mistake or distorts the picture, then perhaps advice is helpful. But if you repeat the advice and the action continues without result, I advise you not to worry about how many people are committing this distorted action for group identity. I do not need to complain or go to the manager of the place to inform them of what is happening. A manager of any place is not enough to look at complaints, but also to monitor and review what is happening. A good manager usually does not need complaints, as they have monitors and random samples they review in addition to going through those complaints.

And here I return and remind you, who you are, what do you want, and whether the existence in that institution serves your goals...

I remind you of a situation and I apologize for the American style in the previous lines, as the matter really cannot bear argument...

Imagine that you go to an institution and submit a paid service request...

And a polite and respectful employee receives the request from you and receives the exact amount of money without any increase, then hands it over to the person in charge of implementation, and what do you want described in a complete, engineered, and organized paper...

This person places your paper on top of the one filled with your orders and those of other clients, as he stumbles around the company, he accidentally drops your paper, perhaps spilling tea on it by mistake instead of returning it to you, feeling ashamed and ignoring the matter.

You are waiting for someone from the institution to call you to agree with you and set a date to do what you requested, while your request lies in the trash, after some time you return to find that the paper is no longer there, and the mistake-making employee may be present or not.

Will you blame the company or the mistake-making employee or the respectful employee who did his job..

Of course, the entire institution, perhaps even to blame this poor employee who did his role perfectly, in reality, it is not his mistakes, but because he is part of a failing institution.

What about the manager ...?

Maybe he will tell you to fill out your order again ...?

This is not enough for the thief, dear, if he knew that when he is stopped he pays back what he stole and goes, he will repeat, and the mistake when he faces punishment will repeat either through negligence or forgetfulness

And you, the victim, are not for your mistake but because you are a part of the collective identity that is distorted by that bad employee

Therefore, always remember, dear one, you are not compelled to stay here

Perhaps your mistake is not because you are wrong, but because you were with the collective identity mistake, and maybe even because you tried to advise them; they will make a mistake and accuse you of doing the same...

And perhaps I should remind you of the situation of this nurse Sarah who said in one of her videos that she was infected by a contaminated needle after someone else left it in the hospital without putting it in the designated place for the wrongdoer, and who is affected by this...?

Arrogance in Advice

Maybe you stand and repeat this sentence: "The person who wrote this book advised himself with it, or as it is said in Arabic, and if I am ashamed to mention it in text, but why not look at the look of a man who made a mistake and wants no one else to make the same mistake?

What he made is why not look at that look or perhaps less than that, to take the information and analyze it logically and see for yourself what I advise you. I do not mean myself, but the advice is general.

Arrogance towards advice does not mean rejecting it because accepting or rejecting advice is up to you, and we cannot accept all the advice that comes to us, as we mentioned, because even the good example you follow will find a lot of difference between you and him in your way of life and his way of life, and your circumstances and his circumstances.

But I mean the arrogance towards advice by mocking it and not reading it or your sentence to the speaker, "Next time, next time, or I'm busy, or I'm not free for your empty words."

Perhaps to be honest, advice is sometimes like a friend who calls you to scold you for leaving the table with your friends in the restaurant because you have something more important... We will talk about that in detail in the chapter on priorities.

But the most important idea is to listen to advice and understand it, not to talk more than to speak, but to speak as little as possible.

The advice was not only that of the spoken word, but perhaps as is the case in books and novels...

What matters is that you remember, dear, who you are and what you want, what are your goals and what are your steps, and listen and read, then decide which ones suit you and which do not, but remember that it is not better for you to curse an advisor for their advice than for the advisor themselves, for those who take advice are more likely to have made many mistakes because with every mistake, they offer an honest advice based on a real experience.

And the successful people may advise you, but taking advice from those who have succeeded will only lead you to repeat their projects and methods sometimes, and sometimes this is not required, and the most strange is that many of them will be preoccupied with their own projects, and finally, most of them have not experienced those mistakes that they advise you to avoid, from which they have fallen...

However, advice from both those who succeed and those who fail will benefit you if you decide when to use each of them accurately and appropriately

Delivering advice as axioms...

Perhaps you wanted to emphasize this point here and then after a point that accepts the advice or, in other words, rejects the advice as a cause of failure

I wanted to emphasize that taking advice as axioms is also a cause of failure

What if the person who advises you or the book you read was living at a different social level or era, and they are talking to you in the language of their time, thought, and status? You might remember that those advices seem strange, as a European human in those cold environments might need fuel for heating most of the time, while you use a fan or air conditioner for cooling.

The thought is different, and the advice may not fit you and your goals.

Let me give you an example from the medical field; I am one of those who study nursing.

Sometimes the symptoms on the patient are the same and the signs are the same, and you find that the medicine is opposite.

Advice from a doctor to a patient who is unconscious after measuring blood sugar, possibly a dose of glucose and possibly a dose of insulin.

With other medications, I won't go into detail; the matter here is not a joke, the symptoms are similar. You see the advice of someone who said "happened like this and did like this and it worked," while the same symptoms, if you did the same thing with them, would be deadly.

Take the advice as a call to understand and think, not a neural signal from a source that cannot be stopped, it moves on its own.

You are a human being, remember that you have a different idea and goal, and you are aware of what you want to do. You have a plan, you have motivation, you have things similar to others. Everyone has a goal, but you have differences in those steps, the method, the style, the circumstances, and also the time...

Oh dear, listen to the advice, think about it, and reflect on yourself. The decision is yours alone, and so is the responsibility. Success is yours alone, and so is failure too.

Emotional thinking

One of the causes of failure related to not knowing who you are and what you want, as well as what affects you, such as emotions. Perhaps the two most emotional influences on us humans are the emotions of hate followed by the emotion of love.

Perhaps that emotion is more prevalent in women and perhaps it is more between the different genders.

Talked about this topic in one of my books, mentioning the Arabic book "Principles of Modern Thought Control" and its English edition, also titled "ABC of ABC."

But let's take it back when we think and make decisions, go and come back, propose an idea, make a judgment, and take advice; there are many emotions within us that affect us, for example, if a person you hate advises you and you refuse his advice, it is not because you hate him, but because you are avoiding his advice.

Or on the other hand, when a beautiful girl invites you to do something that is not necessarily right, and you do it just out of your emotions towards her...

The heart pumps blood into our blood vessels, and it is also the source of our emotions.

Imagine how many decisions you have made with your emotions

How many times have you stopped a decision because of your emotions or accepted it because of your emotions? I'm not giving examples here because I'm sure you have done a lot and can count them, and I have also done so

So, my dear, the next time you make a decision, do not stop at your emotions. This will not happen. Instead, reconsider with a rational perspective. Measure your success and failure. When you go for marriage, set the standards you are looking for, otherwise, you will be overwhelmed by your emotions. We are in that period from the age of eighteen to thirty-six, and any person of the opposite sex will win our hearts with a smile or a smile

As for emotions in work, I may remind you of this image

Actress in a man extinguishing fire and a policeman going to find the place on fire and sitting down to greet each other

The matter may seem strange, but it happens in many forms within institutions and companies

Many times, you find that employees have more friendship and love among themselves than loyalty to the institution itself, and that's why you often find this phrase

"It's our company..... passionate"

This may seem good for both employees, but what about the third one who works properly and integrally when the company's collective identity goes wrong

I am not saying that emotion disappears from companies, but at least it should be the priority for the institution

The blind copying...

I still remind you and end with this title, blind copying as one of the causes of failure that belong to your own ignorance of who you are, what you want, and how similar what you do is to what others do

The strange thing is that it is not essentially welcome to do what others do and that this gear convince yourself that you are an ideal employee in a company and that you are sufficient to do the work properly to advance or to keep your job, of course, this will replace you with a mechanical gear or artificial intelligence tool

But the matter does not end here, even when you go to open a project or start developing yourself. You are used to similarity and imitation

Perhaps I repeat it in a society that encourages this

You go to the elementary in a group, then middle and then secondary class, then you understand that you will think about the college, and you find this person or that prevents you from thinking, but you have to save theories with the names of their saying and complete schedules from a thousand cells just because of a degree is a blind imitation without benefit

This is your creativity and thought, and what is new?

Every time you think of stepping out of the box, you are accused of ignorance and more for just being different.

But it's fine, my dear, if success requires you to be different, then be different. And if society requires you not to be different, then hide your beliefs and ways. If you succeed, announce your success. And if you fail, don't tell them, for they will envy you and blame you and put you in a cycle of failure and disappointment.

Every time you know yourself correctly and answer these questions without haste, take the results away from emotions and take appropriate advice, hide your beliefs and avoid showing your difference, even if you do.

I do not say that you succeed, but that at least you will not repeat the mistakes of others ..

Chapter Two

This chapter discusses the reasons for failure related to the environment, and perhaps I did not delve into it further because I am firmly convinced that successful institutions and individuals can do so even in corrupt environments despite the difficulties. But let's say that these reasons include a demoralizing environment, ranging from corruption to social corruption, through randomness and favoritism, lack of resources, collective monopoly, and the inability to accept unjustified interference in privacy.

Perhaps many of the reasons for the failure related to the environment, but I focused on the most important reasons that are difficult to overcome, and you should avoid being present in them. As for others, a person can overcome it and even benefit from it.

The frustrated environment ..

I am not talking about the spatial environment here, but the components of the environment, people who are a source of failure by their disappointment in you all the time, by a word or an action, or even by their style

I still remember that person in the work environment somewhere who once told me, when I asked him about his opinion on a proposal, "It's not helpful at all"

I was not asking about the possibility; I already had the way. So I sat down to discuss with him, and he argued with me, "It's not helpful at all"

Then, when I presented the idea to his colleague, it was accepted and appreciated, and it started to be implemented and ended, and I sent them the work, but the environment is discouraging, I don't say an individual is discouraged

The same person who rejected the idea, as if he dealt with it emotionally, saying "The idea will not succeed as long as you reject it in the first place."

And here he goes for month after month without reviewing the work under the excuse of time.

Until the work ended with nothing, and to avoid conflict and argument, I ended my existence in such an environment...

Perhaps I mentioned it to you before and I repeat it.

Yes, we live on Earth and not in heaven

Here there is frustration, injustice, and a bad environment, but it's okay, you are capable despite that because the problems of the frustrating environment are not in front of you only but in front of everyone, and it is one of the shared things in most cases of failure

And the solution is usually

Escape...

And leave that frustrating environment

Perhaps you will decide on a challenge and an experiment, but the frustration in the environment is not just for one or two people, but it is a complete framework. When it began, it became a repetitive state; this frustrates this and that flatters this

In such an environment, merely proposing becomes impossible and even if the implementation is perfect, there will be flaws in it

I still remember those who I told to use QR technology for communication and to request the number, and they replied boldly and ignorantly, "What if there's no internet...?!"

Just being around such people turns you from someone who tries to someone who is discouraged and from someone who criticizes to someone who sees the matter as natural

From someone who invents the light bulb to someone who sees that candles are more commonly used, therefore they are right

It is a discouraging environment, and the best advice is to leave, you are not a tree

Societal corruption

Viewing corruption as one of the causes of failure related to the environment, it can be defined as a state of intellectual and moral collapse within society where the predominant opinion turns into disbelief, and deviation and eccentricity from the norm into audacity. The word 'opinion' means betrayal, the word 'thought' means disbelief, and 'no worse than murder.' The loud, unexplained voices turn into nature, and personal matters into humiliation.

Here, it is difficult to say that this is a cause of failure because it is simply a haven that prevents any success and considers every idea as dangerous and every change as an outcast and every attempt as foolish and despicable.

Here, you see the corruption of environmental morality represented by hypocrisy. This was my beloved, and as soon as he left, you hear 'From him to God, the others upon us.' And the other, Mostafa, was my beloved, and as soon as he left, 'Mostafa is the worst human being...'

This is moral corruption; as for intellectual corruption, perhaps that sentence is the worst you have ever heard when I once proposed an idea to a colleague, and he said, 'Don't change the system of the place.'

This state of disorder seems like a heavenly order that does not interfere

Then these loud voices, perhaps you look at them and see them as moral corruption, but I also look at those loud voices without reason as a waste of energy, intellectual corruption, distraction of the audience, and insult to the present. It also reduces the community identity of the place

But what about that popular singer whose voice rises in the space and two pieces of bread, a young man, and a closed door...

No, I don't look at him as moral corruption, even though it is also intellectual corruption, a waste of time for the actors and the present, and the reputation of the place is also wasted

Here, this is not the cause of failure as I spoke, but a breeding ground for it and a fertile environment.

But what is the cause of failure in social corruption if...

The reason here is to be in an environment like this and think that you can improve it or modify it as you try to sweeten the sea water. Perhaps it is possible theoretically and theoretically, but it is not practically possible and basically you do not need to do this because you can simply do the one solution in such problems related to the environment that cause failure.

Leave the environment and go to another...

Where righteous companions guide you instead of this bringing you down and belittling you, and it may even go as far as hating you and plotting against you, just as it happened with Prophet Lot.. "Drive them out of your town, for they are a corrupt people who purify themselves."

Remember, my brother, for you may now know who you are, what your goals are, what you want to do, and what your plan is....?

Then, if your plan depends on place and people, change it, or in either case, leave that corrupt environment.

Randomness

One of the causes of failure related to the environment is randomness, which is that state of the non-planned and possibly non-systematic system where boundaries in dealing are blurred and people ignore or are unaware of the purpose of their presence in the place and the purpose of their cooperation.

Here, as mentioned, a person can spill tea on a client's paper and instead of asking for a copy, ignore it and claim that they did not receive it. Here, a person can do something and forget about it, and another comes and does the same thing, and all of them spend a full day at work and find them complaining that time is not enough.

Here, a simple request from a person to send a message before calling becomes a crime, and naming files with headings becomes a waste of time.

Here, saying to a person in the work environment "Do not walk quickly or run aimlessly inside the place" becomes a misdemeanor.

Here words meet and titles fade, not out of respect for the heart, but because each one sees the honor of the other as an insult to themselves, turning the word "Your Honor" into an insult.

Here are people of professions that no one knows about.

This is the case for institutions, but for individuals, the randomness of the environment differs.

That person you see with disorganized files on their phone.

And you see the messages he sends to others, each message edited 20 times, one message in five messages

The randomness of the environment means the absence of order in life, it gives you a date that it sets and then does not come and forgets so and so and starts with so and so

The personal randomness is a fact that cannot be explained, just the name itself indicates it

And it is one of the reasons for failure

Partisanship

One of the reasons for failure present in environments that can be traditionally defined as supporting and serving relatives and acquaintances more than the general public, whether in employment or directing services. On the other hand, the partisanship that is meant to be mentioned here is the favoritism towards the ideas of relatives and followers and supporting their ideas and opposing those who disagree with them merely because they are followers, not more...

Here, partisanship is not a factor or cause of failure for those who live in an environment suffering from partisanship, but also for the person who flatters someone with partisanship and takes their opinion and supports them, they may also fail for this reason...

Imagine if a public employee worked to appoint one of their relatives to a company with partisanship, and this appointed person made many mistakes. This would be a reason for viewing him poorly as an employee because he was responsible for this foolish person...

This is in good companies, but in companies that suffer from corruption, the manager and employees might be colleagues from the same batch or nephews or nieces, and no one will be held accountable, and no one will look or review...

But what is the pivotal point that causes failure in nepotism?

Simply, it is the inequality of opportunities in place, so it won't matter how hard you work, or how many ideas you come up with, or how you strive for advancement.

The most important is the manager's brother or relative.

Perhaps nepotism has another meaning other than kinship, which is the nepotism of thought.

Some people tend to support those who agree with them rather than those who provide good work.

Here the most important thing is for nepotism to be this favoritism and loyalty, knowing that the person who objects to me is right.

But it doesn't matter to you really.

The most important thing is that you find agreement with like-minded individuals or favoritism towards relatives, and then you know that you are in the wrong place to develop yourself and unleash your thoughts and creativity

Take the first exit and escape from that environment

Lack of resources

As one of the environmental causes of failure, at a certain level it becomes a cause of failure, but before this level, it can be overcome. For example, perhaps desert environments with rain can be cultivated, but what about without rain?

This is the closest example, imagine if you worked in a company that does not provide internet or computers or even an elevator, maybe a laptop would suffice, but what if the environment does not provide a bathroom or water or even a shaded place? What if transportation is not provided?

When we talk about the gap level between resource shortage as a cause of failure and resource shortage as one of the challenges, this level differs from one culture to another and from one work environment to another.

Here I am not telling you to leave the place, but at least never give up trying. As long as there is no other environmental reason, you can continue and reach your goal, whether as an institution or as an individual, with a lot of creativity and a little patience...

Collective Monopoly

This simply means that all individuals within the environment agree on a single thought or opinion regarding a specific issue and monopolize all objections to it, whether they are objections of thought or idea. In doing so, they prevent discussion and belittle anyone who approaches this subject or objects to it, and perhaps they may accuse or plot against them for their objection. Unfortunately, in this case, they will succeed because the best solution to most environmental problems is to speak out. You don't face an individual who can be convinced, but the opinion of the group unites in this monopoly. The other solution, as I mentioned earlier, is to conceal your opinion, but you must realize that any attempt to express your opinion on that idea will be met with monopoly until you can prove your point, and then you can confront. But, my dear, opt for the first solution, for even after you have succeeded in proving your point, it is not enough because all the cunning will be upon you, and here the monopoly turns and becomes one of the causes of failure.

Not accepting objections.

The environment that refuses objections is a rigid, backward environment. If Edison had not objected to the candles, he would not have invented electricity.

Had he not objected to me, the global judiciary, Interpol, and others would not have existed

The objection and presenting the problem is the first step and the first steps of change

Here in this environment that rejects objections, you might hear words like "What's the matter with you to stop it?"

Or "Are you inventing?"

As if the world around us would stop progressing unless we advance and innovation is a burden

As if people have considered the current situation as something divine, some even refuse to understand that change and protest will be in their own interest

Even to the extent that some may decide to plug their ears to any protest simply because they are immersed in the environment around them and no longer see the importance of change, they are closed off within themselves as if they cannot change anything

The strange idea is that the protester does not mean by his protest that he rejects the existing system entirely, but rather that he may want a simple, thoughtful modification

The matter here is mere stagnation and backwardness, and a desperate attempt to maintain the job out of fear of development that would reduce his work.

Perhaps one day I presented an idea to a colleague and received an odd response.

"What are we going to do, anyway?"

The problem was that you simplified the work to a lack of the required action, although they were complaining all the time about its loss.

Despite the intention of that attempt to preserve the status and role of the employee in the face of development, it sometimes leads to the collapse of the entire institution, and here all its employees lose their jobs, and here you find that this is a cause of the failure of institutions

But the matter is different at the individual level

Here, the matter resembles the refusal of advice and the rigidity of thought

All you need, dear, to avoid this cause of failure is to avoid this environment that does not accept objections and at least accepts advice, if only to provoke it and understand it

And those who reject the discussion around you may see it as a sign of intellectual corruption for you and perhaps discourage you...

Unjustified interference in privacy

While I was sitting, suddenly someone stood next to me and looked at my computer screen and asked me, "What are you doing.....?"

I didn't find an answer because I closed the screen and nothing happened

Privacy is not just your phone screen, but also this person who calls you and says things that don't matter, and if you tell them you're busy, you hear their question "What are you doing ...?"

Interfering with privacy might be a colleague asking their colleague to answer "Why do you wear the veil, it's outdated," and interfering with privacy might be a call where you find someone discussing it with you at the end of the call

Interfering with privacy sometimes can be by getting too close

It's true that I don't understand how the two genders get so close to less than a meter and a half and start hitting each other and chasing each other around

It's various forms of intrusion into privacy as a cause of failure, but the focal point is not that anyone is intruding on your privacy, but when this epidemic reaches you and when you are busy monitoring it and asking about its condition and personality and caring about its details

Dear

Whether to avoid the environment or not is not a direct cause of failure, but beware of getting infected. Always remember who you are, what you want, and what your steps and tasks are; you don't need to be busy with others' situations

In the end, my dear, remember that the problems of the environment are difficult to confront and most of them are the case of leaving it without controversy, knowing that the problems that are not mentioned often are possible to deal with them even if it slows down and is inhibited by success and makes failure closer to the occurrence, but it will not be a basic cause

Chapter Three

This chapter discusses the tenth habits that cause failure, because these habits are in themselves as reasons that prevent your success starting with the closure of the ear or talk more than listening and reading and ending with a lot of complaint and criticism through relying on memory in the plans and the obscene tongue and the speed of anger and the speed of conclusion, urgency and awakening Recently, without justification, routine, optimism, peasants, or emotionalism in expecting, and discussing positions in every reason and how this reason is prevented from achieving your goal

Close the ear

Closing the ear as a cause of failure is a very widespread phenomenon these days, perhaps many do not think and no longer listen to advice or read or listen to others under the guise of experimentation and error, but by God, how old are you to spend on experimentation and error ...?

How much time do you have to try everything yourself ...?

The matter is like the impossible, for it is not possible for a person to decide to stop learning from others

A situation comes to mind that I will never forget when someone told me, when I explained something simple to him, I am a graduate of College S

I don't know what it means, does it mean that he is a college graduate, or does it mean that he is more than advice, or does it mean that he is older than learning, or that he should take advice from someone younger than him? Perhaps the error was in the style, but certainly, closing one's ears, stopping reading and listening, and diving into others' experiences to learn from them is one of the steps to success. Not just their failed steps, but every step where a person loses or fails, you should learn from them. The successful person is characterized by his habits of reading, learning, asking questions, and listening.

I am not saying that he should implement it, but at least benefit from the experiences of others. Perhaps what he wants to do has been done by others. Perhaps he is thinking of a project that has been established, or perhaps he will find a more beneficial idea for developing his project.

If learning and listening were only done by the ignorant, then the hoopoe would not have said to Solomon, "You have reached what you did not reach."

Man spends his life learning. The more aware a person becomes, the more he realizes how little knowledge there is in this vast universe.

What is the problem that leads to failure ...?

It is your inability to listen to others in their ideas and explanations

The solution is to try and increase your listening time and then think about which ones to implement and which ones do not suit you

Too much complaining and criticism..

Excessive complaining and criticism are one of the worst habits, and someone might ask, "How can I not object to this ignorance and remain silent about this backwardness...?"

The matter is simple as an idea because when you object in an environment where this idea prevails, first of all, no one will care about your objection, but the majority sees your objection as foolish, and perhaps the majority are involved in what they are in, social corruption, maybe they agree with it, and maybe they are afraid to talk as you might be afraid of exposing them to intellectual monopoly.

Simply, intelligent people value their ideas well, either to implement them and surprise everyone or to hide their beliefs and coexist in peace with this environment without achieving success or failure in silence.

And the failures either fade away in thought and forget their ideas, goals, and principles or speak out loud and expose themselves to monopoly, and then they fail because the most severe form of social punishment returns on them in that corrupt environment within the institution.

But on a personal level, a person who is constantly complaining wastes their time instead of trying to find solutions. They waste time on complaints that will never calm you down. Instead, be silent and embark on a profound silence until you achieve what you seek, as long as this serves your thought and ideology.

But complaining and criticizing loudly, whether it is for individuals or institutions, will not benefit anyone except in a negative way, and often the complainers are subjected to revengeful attacks and drink from the cup of artificial, decorated problems with trivialities.

Or they may be subjected to methods of humiliation or possibly face complaints in return for their own complaints.

Ask yourself what I want ...? Who am I ...? And how do I execute ...? And whether complaining will achieve my desires ..?

Will anyone move or only, as some say, barking while the convoy is going in the opposite direction .... And since those complaints fall in the habits area, with time, your criticism and your complaints will turn to elaborate silence, you usually work in silence without doubt and invest your time in the solution, not complaining or leave The institution that you complain about in silence also ..

Dependence on memory on plans.

How many times did you say you plan to do something great and did not do ...

How many times have you sat with yourself and said you will get a training course and forgot ...

How many times did you wake up early to do many tasks and found yourself at 2 PM holding your phone and browsing Facebook...?

And how much of this and that...? And how many times did you take an appointment with someone and forget about visiting them..?

The human memory is short and weak, and the truth is that this is a feature that gives you a chance to get rid of problems and psychological stress, but when it comes to planning and answering this question about yourself who you are and what your goals are, or even for institutions in relation to their vision and mission

things become catastrophic

When you are without a plan, you are more prone to waste time, at least because you do not remember the length of time you are doing something, and sometimes because you are always squeezing yourself to do and do and finish, and the hour has passed five and the

here you must have your plans written down and your information about yourself recorded or written down, even if it is electronic on your phone, so that you can return to it

Do not forget the day my friend gave me a book titled Sales Psychology. I learned from it to write my plans, and now I am writing a book, which is the fourth in my series, within a plan that has lasted for two years

I remember that I often forget the plan or deviate from it, but because I wrote a plan that includes a vision and a mission and general goals for my life, and I set 200 goals for my life over the next two years, here I am just finishing or supervisor to finish the first year, and now I have completed 70% of the goals...

I don't think I could have achieved them without writing down a plan.

Every time I feel bored with my life, I go back to it and see how much I have achieved of my goals, and it makes me feel better.

And every month, I set a group of goals to work on.

I have divided my tasks as usual into four layers: the first "A" level is urgent and important and must be done, and the last one is not urgent and not important, and I usually only do it for leisure.

The second one is important but not urgent, and the third one is urgent but not important

But beware in the layer of important but not urgent that leaving it behind and neglecting it may turn into urgent and important at some point

The most important thing about the topic is to relax your mind, organize your life, and write down your ideas so that you can return to them when you want or after you have let them go

And at the end of each day, set your goals for the next day to do them; maybe you won't complete them, but it's fine because you tried and didn't waste time as you used to

the offensive tongue

One of the habits that lead to failure is the offensive tongue or, in other words, the rude manner, whether in disagreement or even in humor

Here I do not mean hypocrisy in speech is good, but simply the difference is always clear from a person's style in speaking. You may have heard someone say, "This person has insulted me in a polite manner"

Yes, you can always scold and ask questions, make objections and complaints, but in a good manner. I am not saying that the author of the book does this, but it is a very difficult skill, but many people have mastered it, which means that you can also do this

The malicious tongue may turn gentle speech into cursing and turn humor into insult, making some avoid speaking with you from the outset. And perhaps this is necessary sometimes, but in reality, most often it leads to failure, monopoly, a bad reputation, and avoiding communication with you, and sometimes even complaining about you. I'm not saying you should be insincere, but rather rely on ambiguity if you can, where you criticize and expose that you are flattering. There is always a style I recommend, though I don't excel at it myself, and that is the art of wrapping. When you start your speech with praise and flattery for the person, then reveal the problem and the objection, and then cover it up with more praise and flattery...

Here, you avoid the malicious tongue as a cause of failure, and at the same time, you can deliver criticism smoothly.

But why is the malicious tongue a cause of failure for people...?

Simply because no one wants to hear a sentence saying they are wrong.

For if you can wrap it or hide it if you prefer to hide it, in either case, be careful with sweet talk, especially with managers, and let me tell you something of utmost importance

People like to talk simply and sincerely with those who are less knowledgeable than themselves, so whenever you show your ignorance to people, advise them with what they have, and attack you with their knowledge of what they know and from their ignorance what they reveal in their words, and perhaps I am not good at this either...

It seems that I will benefit from this book like you, dear, in improving my style of communication and avoiding the nastiness of the tongue

Speed of anger...

Perhaps it is important for the matter to be at the beginning of the chapter, but it is fine here.

Speed of anger is one of the worst habits that lead to failure.

Here, we do not just look at the speed of anger as a result of stressful situations in the life of the idea or even in your personal life, but also the speed of anger due to not achieving the desired results quickly.

You are thinking today about a solution to an emerging problem and want a good result tomorrow or even talk to someone who listens to your words and becomes angry and forgets that the idea is still being implemented step by step. This does not mean at all that if you take steps, results will appear in every step. Many understand that during the construction of the zodiac, the first steps are plans on paper that do not appear, but the digging does appear, but it can be in the opposite direction of the construction. Then, laying the foundations, which are the most burdensome and least visible, and then the roles begin to appear. Do you understand how this process works in any plan?

Do you really understand how and when the results can appear, or will you collapse and forget everything you have done at the first setback and the first objection to your idea?

Perhaps the hardest thing is that you are not alone in making plans, perhaps you are making plans to create a project, and before you start the implementation, you find another one who has started a similar one...

Here, you should go back and think again, or even cooperate with it as a partner if possible, or maybe start in another place

Anger does nothing but waste time here

Do you have to return to your plan and ideas and your identity from yourself? And what do you want...? And is what you want possible to be implemented with other ideas and thoughts...?

Dear

The speed of anger is no more than an escape from reality and the forgetting of your essence and the essence of your basic ideas and the transformation from a human being with real goals in growth to a person who knows himself as an engineer or a doctor or the owner of a project when he failed in this went and cried as if he created a doctor or an engineer or an owner of a project

Reschedule your entry and reschedule your thinking and start not to say something new but from where you ended

speed of inference

What if a person is greeted with peace and does not respond? Is he a pirate from you or a flaw in you...? Or maybe he didn't hear you or something else...?

Scientists believe that the response of a person and their reactions depend more on them than on the action and the doer

Therefore, hasty conclusions are often a habit that often leads you to failure because simply with your first mistake, you will be disappointed and perhaps the opposite with your first success, you will leave and be overjoyed, without having completed your project, but only achieved progress

The rapid conclusion as one of the reasons for failure means taking insufficient meanings to expect a result that may be a tragic result that makes you feel shameful with your first failure. For example, if you set a daily plan and it is not pleased with what is fine, this is normal in the beginning, you are trying something that you have not accustomed to days after you will know how many tasks you expect that Do and reduce the time you are wasted, perhaps the first of you is that you have decided to plan for your life, and this is in itself a success that does not do it, but many do not know it.

It is also related to good listening

I often read in the book and I find the writer forget something and I would like to mention it, then it is only the lines and I find the writer talking about it and perhaps doing and vilifying those who do this thing that I was waiting for

Just be patient and you will find what you want and will happen what I planned here because I am talking about habits.

Perhaps the habit clung to you until you became the other one who clung to it, and it became a habit or was created by you and became part of your character.

But the advantage is also that even though it is difficult to change a habit, whenever you created it, it will continue with the difficulty of forgetting it.

When did you learn not to rush to conclusions, not to rush to anger, or to hurry the results? Those habits may continue with you forever and will not become a cause of your failure again...

Waking up lately without a reason

I liked to confirm that there is no justification for the back waking up to be one of the reasons for failure. Perhaps someone looks and says I am doing nursing, doctor or others. I have to work at night. This is a natural work and I cannot change it, but in any case, waking up recently without justification. This is one of the reasons for the failure associated With customs because you simply when you are used to not standing from your sleep at the beginning of the day, your will is absent in change and planned work. What if you sleep and do without a date ...

And what if your life goes to work and goes back and sleeps, then wakes up late, and you will return to work again.

What a tired routine is a tired routine just to think about it ....!

When did you develop yourself ... and when you work and when you plan to get out of your place as an Elect in a factory to a gearmaker

Decide possibly to change the production line and the method of work, or perhaps to own a factory

There is no doubt that this requires time, and therefore, you waste your time and do not have enough time for planning and development

Someone might say, "Why don't I come back from work and make the plan in the evening...?"

Never, never, and how can you plan after implementation...!

Your work during working hours also requires a plan, otherwise you will return from work and the manager will have assigned you tasks that you have not completed, and you will spend your night completing them.

And with your inability to develop yourself, simple tasks become difficult work that requires hours or even days.

And any work done at night also requires a greater number than usual.

How, and time is time...?

Simple time is what it is, but focus is not what it is

So you go to bed late and wake up late without any reason, wasting hours of your mental activity in routine tasks that do not require the level of focus and planning that the work needs to develop yourself in the morning

Because you did not set a sleep schedule and you did not set a plan for what you will do during the day, perhaps a colleague at work invites you to a dinner party or an activity, and you leave your work to develop yourself or plan your future to go with them and forget everything about who you are..? What do you want ..? And about your plan to get out of this rut ..? And the role you play, if you do not let go of self-improvement, it will let you go by replacing you with an artificial intelligence tool or another employee who can do better than you and improve the results

Or even an artificial intelligence robot or a mechanical system in the factory

Therefore, dear one, stop working randomly, sleeping without a schedule, and talking without action. Stop making unplanned plans. As long as you can wake up a few hours before work, make a plan to plan your day and decide which hours of the day you will spend on self-improvement and which tasks are of grade "A" and which are of grade "B", "C", or "D" so you can focus on important tasks and exclude unimportant and non-urgent tasks.

Today is what it is, and others will spend it. The difference is that you consume the active hours of your mind in routine tasks and plan in hours when your mind's activity is reduced. Although this is enough to reduce your activity and distract your mind, without a plan in the morning, you often forget to sit and think in the evening, and the cycle continues... Did you understand why waking up late without a valid reason is one of the causes of failure?

Routine

Routine is simply falling into repetitive cycles of traditional routine and turning from a person who develops themselves into someone who spends the whole day working.

Perhaps you earn every dollar work hour today and this invites you to work 18 hours a day and thus you achieve the money you want and this is good but what after a year or two

Here there is another person or people who worked 12 hours and developed themselves in six hours a day, instead of doing what you do in an hour like you

They do it in half an hour

They are now earning in 12 hours as if they were working 24 hours while you are working 18 hours as you can work 24 hours

It is simply the routine, whether you work for money or work for yourself in your institution, work is a certain time and allocate time to develop yourself will work to increase your salary for the longest run other than the routine

The routine will work for you to give you a lot now, but this is a lot that will remain throughout your life

Perhaps your competitor, who earns in the 12 hours of work for what you need to work 24 hours to earn it, reduce what is required of a reward for each project or until the workers in the field increase, so the service makers increase and the salary rate decreases in value, so you find yourself no longer get what you have received despite the The same hours are she works, which is the maximum limit

In short, the routine is to transfer your life to work only for money without developing yourself

Self-improvement is the real investment, which comes from stepping out of the routine of work

Here I am not telling you to quit your job, but you have 24 hours a day that you need 6 hours of sleep and to work daily for a maximum of 12 hours

If you allocate five hours, five days a week or more or less, to improve yourself and learn something new

I am not just talking about knowledge, but about the edge of knowledge or what is called meta-science, and therefore after a period of time, the knowledge in you will accumulate instead of needing to work hours, you will need less and you will have more time, even though you are earning more than you used to, and this is the investment in oneself

In the world of business or work, if you spend your entire life working, the time you spend doing it is the length of your life. But by investing in yourself, you can work ten times your life and be at rest because you understand a function in Excel that might save you hours every day, logging customer phone numbers, and another function allows you to collect millions of fees

With the advent of artificial intelligence, you can accomplish the work of days and, with the tools in the world of intelligence, you work little and produce a lot. Whether you do or do not, others will do. If you do not develop yourself and get out of your repetitive routine, you will die in sorrow for the time you wasted in not developing yourself.

Optimism and Pessimism

Optimism and pessimism, although they are contradictory, are the two sides of the same coin called the avoidance of moderation in expectations.

When I tell you, you need self -development and go to the development of yourself and after a week you learn and increase your productivity, you can never optimistic about all optimism and decide to leave your work a month for self -development because you will turn into an Einnashin or that after a week of working to develop yourself, you have not achieved anything, so look at yourself with remembrance and decide Continue to work as you do without developing yourself pessimistic about what is happening

Optimism and penetration have many examples as a reason for failure, but I mentioned this example because you may remember it from the previous part

Let's imagine that you produced a new product in an oven for baked goods and people.

Or do you gradually add to its production and decide according to production and follow -up every day, whatever it produces every day

The matter here is simple; every day you need to look and review and take your measurements. Do not look at the line of success or failure; they are as they are now. But your actions and changes and changes in the surrounding environment change the curve of your success and failure.

Take measurements before making a judgment and work your logic before working your heart.

Results are based on work and reviews.

Take real opinions from people and study market demands.

Data collection methods as we said in Meta Sciences

You need to continuously review your thoughts, what you have achieved, and what you have failed at without rushing for results; as long as you are working, you will definitely reach your goal. I am talking about working with a plan and thinking, not just standing against a wall. Maybe you can move it...

Chapter 4

This chapter may be the shortest because it mainly discusses one cause of failure, which is not defining or being unable to define priorities in your life. Both have a greater impact than the other, as you may find that there is a conflict between two or more reasons when you make a decision between them. If you do this, you have reduced one of them, and therefore it was necessary for you to understand which one has priority.

At the beginning of the chapter, let's divide what you do in your life into two categories: work that brings you a direct monetary return, such as working in a job or a similar type of work, and other work that develops yourself, which brings you a monetary return indirectly because it simply increases your ability to perform conventional work in a job.

Maybe the question here is which one is more important ...?

One guesses the work that brings a direct monetary return or even the work that develops you because it increases your ability

But it is a dishonest question, for both are important, and the most important is to balance between them and find a balance in both side by side

But how do we divide work into priorities ...?

Perhaps there are more than one way

Perhaps the most famous method is the four-quadrant method, divided into four squares, each containing the intersection of the importance column with the urgency row

Let the work be urgent and important, and it belongs to class "A" and has the highest priority

Important but not urgent, with the second priority and grade "B". Urgent but not important, with the third priority and grade "C". At the end of the matrix, not urgent and not important, it is grade "D".

So how do you navigate your life between these layers of priorities and which one is more important in your life...?

Truthfully, despite the fact that the first priority is the urgent and important grade "A", focusing on what is important in your life and not just what is urgent is the best choice.

Because if you forget grade "B", you will move to grade "A" with time when its time comes.

But regarding the third and fourth grades, j and d, understanding is not very important, so for d, you might want to reduce it to the minimum or even ignore it.

As for j, you can delegate it to someone or even buy an artificial intelligence tool to do it.

If we say that attending class lectures is urgent and important at 8 am, then waking up at 7 or even 4 will be important but not urgent because at this time you will start planning your day and lay out your full plan for the day and after the lecture. This planning may not seem urgent as you think, but it is very important as we have mentioned, and therefore it is of the second grade.

Does it mean that planning is less important than attending...?

Don't think about them as important....!

But the difference is in urgency

So presence is related to a time, but planning is not related to a time, therefore

As we said, the important matters that are not urgent are usually the ones with the greatest focus

Then let's imagine that a friend of yours invites you for lunch here, you accept the invitation urgently because it's related to an appointment, but it's not important because you will not benefit from it in the long run. Perhaps it's a good friendship, but it's not important enough to change the plan you set up here this morning. That invitation in the grade is not important.

Let's say you planned at the beginning of your day and allocated half an hour to browse Facebook at the end of the day, then the teacher of the subject informs you that you have an exam tomorrow.

The exam tomorrow is important, but more importantly, it requires the time for studying that you need. Therefore, you might cancel the 30 minutes of Facebook planned to study in it, and then think about additional studying at the beginning of the next day.

Here, the possibility of non-urgent and non-essential events of grade d in your plan to change is a priority.

Do you want to save time by looking at the category d but you don't find enough time after removing all the allocated time for d, think about j where the non-essential but urgent tasks are, such as watching TV or the TV series you are following or others...

And if this is not enough, the last option in front of you is to remove the non-urgent important matters, such as reading a book or learning a new skill and developing yourself in grade b, but it is very difficult to eliminate a task of grade a and replace it with another task of grade a or b or c or definitely d.

It is not possible to eliminate a task from a priority grade for a task in the priority of zil.

Therefore, you always need to distribute your tasks from a, b, c, and d until you need an important task and find something that can be substituted in your day. Another option is to consider the order of tasks in grade a itself.

The degree of urgency of some tasks may be less than others, despite the fact that all of them are urgent and important

What is more important, an urgent and important training course that you have set a deadline for, such as an exam or an unexpected exam decided by a department in the university?

Of course, the course is less important here, despite the fact that all of them are...

But to be honest, avoid places and work environments of this type when decisions are unexpected

I believe that here the idea of priorities has become clear to you

Let's take an example in the opposite direction

If the chapter discusses not understanding priorities as a cause of failure, then how is understanding priorities

Let's say you just woke up from your sleep at 5 in the morning and began to enter your bathroom and pray perhaps or read your prayers

Then I started with breakfast or my Quranic verse

Then I took the plan you put for today... or if you don't remember setting the plan, you start by setting a plan

Today you have your schedule from 8 am to 2 pm

or your lectures

Place it in the schedule with its time and duration and its category from the type

You have a job interview, put it and specify for it a time, place, and duration from the stage

You have a celebration invitation from a non-close colleague

Place it at its time and place and duration from the grade J

You have a book or downloaded it on your phone to read, or perhaps a YouTube course you'll start, put it and rate it from grade B

Then you found a match with a ball or one of your leisure interests that you need to do today, put it in your schedule from grade D

There is not much free time left in your day, just the time for commuting, which is good

I went to work or lectures and found an extra task assigned to me today, which was not in my plan and added two hours of work

Simply eliminate leisure of grade D and joy of grade G

Then what about adding four extra hours to postpone the course in grade Ba for tomorrow

But always think about the environment that exploits your time outside of its designated hours and the manager who demands work from you and absorbs your time, and cannot reduce it with your experience

Think about the corrupt and random environment here..

Maybe you need to leave...

After coming back, I found a moment of leisure. Think about the course, finish your task, think about the celebration you were invited to. Can't you go? Think about entertainment first, and then reschedule for tomorrow. But here, set aside some time to plan your life and develop yourself to take the course.

Make sure you break free from the routine.

Apologize for some time for extra work if possible, otherwise, enter into a daily routine. Keep all your time for urgent and important work and forget to develop yourself, which is the worst thing that can lead to failure...

Chapter Five

This chapter discusses the reasons that lead you to failure and are related to the steps in the implementation of your project or wish or the company's wish if you are talking about the institution of 'Ali, mentioning ten reasons starting from the implementation before planning and ending with the absence of evaluation and taking opinions from the beneficiaries, and what is called the evaluation of the relatives, passing by the absence of the plan from the outset or importing pre-prepared plans and not writing the plans, marginalizing the plans and measurements, and incorrect measurements of the progress, and sometimes unrealistic plans and rigidity of the plans, and the absence of contingency time

Implementation before Planning

Very often, you hear in work environments that sentence "We start and when we get to this point, God will solve it"

I am here and impressed by the sentence, perhaps the matter concerns the finishing touches and the external color of the building, although this color may match a specific architectural shape, it is fine because the fine details can actually be delayed until after the start

But what about the idea of entering into execution before putting in place a comprehensive plan and framework

If you are building a building

Then perhaps you should develop a comprehensive plan until the apartments are delivered to the buyers and maybe carry out maintenance for the building later and contract this with companies from the very beginning

It's strange that some people hear them say "Don't want any problems at first and everything comes in gradually."

Yes, discussions about the end and incompleteness of the project may occur initially, but this will definitely be better than starting the project and then needing to tear down the building.

Or that no one buys it or that you need more time for execution than you think for reasons you haven't thought of.

Starting the implementation without a plan may make you start, but always remember the illusion of success.

Is not the goal to start, is not the goal as a job interview you enter, is not the goal as a customer enters the supermarket and buys from you a product, the important thing is how many of them will consume it instead of returning it

Starting without a plan is deceiving yourself before deceiving others

If you are a contractor and you want to start implementing the architecture without a plan and you say "Just because I've started, everything is just talk"

Imagine how much money you would lose if the building is rejected or you decide to destroy the foundation and pour it again, how much is your loss

This is not just about big things

Imagine you planned to buy a book and read it

Do you know about the contents and chapters of the book

Did you plan to read the table of contents to find out that maybe you don't need to read it, maybe it's for an advanced level and you are a beginner in the field

Carrying out tasks before planning may be a waste of time when you need to backtrack, but sometimes we don't have a choice but to backtrack.

Imagine that you are sailing in the Red Sea and in the middle of the sea, you remember that you don't have enough food or fuel. You might find a sailor who will save you, but you might return only as a still body.

Carrying out tasks before laying out at least the outlines is recklessness.

Imagine that you decided to start a project with a friend without discussing it with a responsible person and another responsible person like this, and you lost the project here. You won't only lose money, but also your friend, and sometimes your reputation.

Let me talk to you sincerely

When each of us starts to implement, adrenaline and dopamine are high

What ....? Project.....?! Shall we start or the phrase "I'm with you, let's implement"?

But after months, the woes begin, who does what and who is responsible and who and who...?

You are afraid of loss at first, even though the loss at first would prevent you from participating and your share would be zero. However, when you participate without a plan and implement without planning, the losses can be greater and you might return empty-handed after paying thousands and wasting time without a friend or partner, frustrated. You might gain experience, but taking risks without planning does not account for the immense amount of danger, and the success rate is lower here.

Therefore, my dear, every time you think of starting, think of the written plan and discuss it well. If possible, sign it, and if necessary, document it or have two witnesses witness it.

Absence of evaluation

Here I am talking about the absence of evaluation as one of the reasons for failure. A situation where you may have set a plan because I can't imagine you would evaluate, and you didn't set a plan from the beginning.

The assessment here means setting measures for the implementation of each step of the project or idea and beginning to measure it to see if the step has been executed or not

Occasionally, it is referred to as quality control assessment, and sometimes in business projects, it is the assessment of buyers, customers, or even clients

Perhaps you need to assess what you have achieved, and perhaps you even need what is called a 366-degree assessment, which is a multi-aspect assessment

But the most important thing is that the assessment should be part of the plan. I may not present a project management method in this book, but you might need it

Here the evaluation has predefined standards for them to be measured later and to determine if you are accomplishing what has been implemented or not

And the absence of evaluation here is one of the causes of failure because simply not having evaluations means you are not sure you have implemented everything needed... Imagine you decided to adopt that building and plan for it, starting with digging and pouring concrete, and forgot to separate the concrete with a waterproofing material

Without the evaluation of each step in the plan, you might forget a step

Planning alone is not enough here, but it cannot be evaluated without a plan. Instead, the plan needs measures sometimes; perhaps in your plan, you intended to fill each of the foundation basins with water to test the insulation material

Perhaps you need to test your writing skills before you say that you have completed an English course, and this should be done by an external entity that lacks bias to ensure the integrity of the evaluation

What if you have an educational institution and you decide to obtain the quality certification ...?

And you have put a plan in place that does not need to measure the plan and ensure its implementation ...?

For example, you have included in the plan an awareness program for students according to quality standards and implemented it

Have you tested the students to ensure their awareness of what you want them to understand...?

Did you set a step in the plan, for example, to find out the students' attendance at the institution

Have you taken a random sample of the students' attendance at the location...?

Did you set a step, for example, to ensure the quality of the communication system

Did you take a random sample to measure the quality duration of the communication and information exchange system...?

Here, every step you put in your development plan, whether as an institution or even individually, you must understand what the appropriate method is to measure it

And the most important thing here is the measurement

I may be a bit strict

This may be disliked by some people about me or even you, my reader

Evaluation is usually not done on everything; you only take a random sample of the lamps to illuminate them for a period to test their average lifespan, while the rest are distributed easily

So the test and evaluation, although I prefer to test all units if possible, just like in testing all car or phone batteries, for example

But in the case of lamps, it is not possible because, as one person told me, you would have to turn them all on and sit next to the lamps until they burn out..

The message is that if this random sample indicates the quality of the rest of the elements, then sometimes you may take a sample and by bad luck, the problem does not exist

Even if the sample is random and with a sufficient percentage of the total number

But the most important and stricter matter, as you said, is what is your response to the discrepancies

If one of the workers or employees makes a mistake

This cannot be said that a random sample proves the inaccuracy of one of the customers' or patients' data, if the only response is that you are asking him to correct it.

He will simply think that.

I make many mistakes, and only a supervisor comes once, and when he discovers an error, he asks when to correct it.

It's hilarious...

Here simply evaluating by the random sample is not useful, but you need to evaluate all elements to ensure their safety and every step by yourself.

But what if this person knows that any mistake discovered will be severely punished, and perhaps he will be reprimanded or his services will be terminated here? He will make sure to improve his work and refine it because he fears that a mistake discovered by him will occur. Here, a random sample will suffice and make sure it is truly random; no one who chooses it is the one who made it. Here, the severity of the punishment is enough to ensure the quality of the product by taking random samples, but I do not say absolute severity, for every mistake has a suitable punishment and decision. The most important thing is that there is a decision made by a larger authority than just "If you allow us, we found a mistake... Correct it...!"

Evaluating relatives and seeking opinions from beneficiaries

Let me discuss with you the first method of evaluation, which is evaluating relatives.

I once registered to study in the Arabi Department of the American People's University, and I was drawn to this new term in the evaluation, which is the evaluation of the peers.

It is simply an evaluation of the work of people like you while they are being evaluated, looking at the right things they do and saying yes, this is something I should do, and looking at the mistakes they make and saying yes, this is something I should avoid...

Let me try this type of peer evaluation with you, for example, when relying on a specific educational institution.

How do you know the form and style of dealing with accredited educational institutions if you haven't tried it yourself?

Evaluating counterparts invites you to visit an authorized institution and observe the atmosphere and system to try to understand the things applied there to transfer them to your own institution. This may sometimes be called learning by apprenticeship or experiencing in a similar environment or external training or even normalization when you try to convince your employees to see the result of the change after the full implementation of the plan. However, here the counterpart evaluation helps you to envision the form of the result to achieve the quality certificate and to imagine the image of the place that has obtained the quality certificate.

The second method is to take opinions from the beneficiaries, which sometimes correspond and sometimes do not. For example, it is difficult to evaluate a teacher by his students or a manager by the one who leads them, although it may happen. However, it is easy in commercial companies to take opinions from customers and clients to ensure the level of customer satisfaction. Here, the level of work efficiency can be measured by the level of customer satisfaction with it.

No matter which method you use, whether through measurements, counterparts, customers, or the 360-degree evaluation that measures all aspects of the evaluation.

Each may be right at times and wrong at others...

absence of the plan from the very beginning

This title I mention here as one of the reasons for failure, but in reality, I started with it in the implementation phase before planning. Without the plan, it is impossible to proceed because evaluation, originally, comes based on a plan and the criteria on which it is evaluated are set during the planning phase.

Importing plans

This matter is closer to failure, but it may succeed

I mean by importing plans, not to put a construction plan based on the spatial, temporal, and surrounding circumstances, but to use a plan that succeeded somewhere and try to copy it elsewhere

This may seem strange

How can importing plans be a cause of failure

How can a large accounting program be designed not to suit a similar institution

The matter may have confused you because the broader plan is to lay out the overall framework with a roadmap for implementation that includes coordinates and execution, and perhaps the names of the implementers here may change, and perhaps some points are detailed as if this happened, then the decision is this, and if the other happened, then the decision is that

And as I said, it may succeed in cases like the WordPress framework

It is a framework for implementing websites

No details of the plan are provided, but you get the framework and complete the details

The difference between the general outline and the detailed information is significant; perhaps the planning steps are the same and the decision-making steps are usually the same, but every plan contains its own specific details

If you set up a plan to build a building in a residential area by importing a building plan for a desert area, it is different

Perhaps the land here is sandy and clayey here, perhaps the workers work in the desert under one work system and in residential areas under another system, perhaps even the transport of goods is by a different system, perhaps even the implementation, where the building is insulated thermally in the residential area is currently not insulated in the desert

The matter actually differs in details

Is the treatment plan for a patient with diabetes or obesity the same for all patients? Although both are patients with diabetes or obesity, the details are definitely different, and perhaps many people see false advertisements

Treatment plan for diabetes - medicine for obesity

As one of the workers in the healthcare sector and after studying nursing for 4 years

There is no treatment without diagnosis, so let's be honest

Treatment can reduce symptoms, all the pain can be alleviated with a combination of painkillers

But what about the cause

Simply, every plan put in place, whether for treatment, building a building, teaching a student English, or even for an institution to obtain a quality certificate, differs

The evaluation may be similar and the purpose may be the same, but the steps, conditions, and factors are different, and therefore the plans are different.

Therefore, think twice before asking your colleague "How can I...?" He may have enough time, and you may be different from him, so the broad strokes in his plan may be helpful, but handling the plan to represent you is more important.

Just because the evaluation of the location was successful in that plan does not mean that the evaluation will be possible for you to achieve quality in the same plan.

Not writing the plans

No meaning for a plan that is not documented. If you don't document the plan, you will definitely forget it. And I don't mean here to write on paper, perhaps electronic or graphical documentation is better, especially with the growth of plans and their components. Not just writing a plan, but announcing it, and making it complete for each specialist in their field, with some general outlines for other disciplines.

Imagine if you were building a building and decided to give the plan to the electrician to implement the wiring and pipes. The electrician doesn't know where the water pipes are; he might shorten some electric locations to water locations, and a disaster might occur.

Imagine if you agreed on a plan and didn't write or announce it.

Is it not possible that someone might forget something and have to delay the implementation...?

This is not only in major projects, but even in a book reading plan

If you do not make a written plan

When do you start reading this chapter and how from ...

You will not start, or maybe you put the plan to read and forget a book

I expect you've done it a thousand times and I'm just like you

The human memory was not created to remember all your plans, otherwise why would God burden the human with learning by the pen, and why would writing not be the greatest discovery

And the celestial books did not depend on the memorizers instead of writing

But here, please note that some plans are written in code or sent and burned, like military and secret plans sometimes

Margin of plans

Margin of plans means not including the precise details in them and it is one of the reasons for failure. Perhaps the margin of plans includes sentences like I will read Ibn Khaldoun's book.

Any book by Ibn Khaldoun and what time is it and is it with you or on the internet and is it benefiting you and how many times a month do you read it.

All of this should possibly be included in the plan.

However, at least include the outlines, or in large projects, the plans may be in the form of folders.

Just assign each person to develop a plan for their specialty, then integrate the comprehensive plan to ensure there is no overlap in time and space, then announce the plans after modification, discuss them with senior specialists to ensure their satisfaction or give them the opportunity to make suggestions for the final modification, and then each of them should receive a detailed copy.

Misjudgments

Are setting wrong measures for success, and thus, an error occurs in the assessment, and sometimes what is called the illusion of success or rushing the steps occurs, for example, by determining that the measure of the success of concrete columns is their height, and neglecting the number of bars and their resistance to loads and the quality of the concrete pouring, for example.

Or sometimes when planning, you don't put someone to measure or there isn't an eligible or trustworthy person to measure, so you hear the phrase "Everything is fine, boss" and "How complete it is," and this has not happened.

Imagine if the person who pours concrete or the person responsible for manufacturing chairs for an institution or the person responsible for sending the sample is the same person responsible for the implementation here; they will send you the best measured sample so that you can trust it and fill out the report based on it, even though they are sure that it does not represent the reality. Therefore, in any project, it is necessary to have the independence and honesty of the assessors, and the successful manager must always take random samples from everything, whether known to the employee or not, and also whether known to the responsible person or not at all times.

So the random sample is the one where every element has an equal chance of being chosen...

As I said, the strictness of punishment for errors in random samples is important because it is difficult to test everything yourself.

Infeasibility of plans

What if you are not proficient in a language and decided to enter an advanced language course directly from the beginner's level to the intermediate and the intermediate to the advanced

Plans are important and it is important that they be written and evaluation is required since the plan is written

But the most important thing is to be realistic, I don't mean realism to stay in the state that everyone lives in, but realism that the plan is logical, even though the condition of realism is often required for any goal

Is the goal really real before defining it ...?

You don't live on the moon or Mars...!

Don't say you're coming with an employee whose salary is S and say give him three times as much to work the whole day instead of spending on transportation costs

I was in one of the factories one day and some of the workers would slack off occasionally, so the supervisor would come and communicate with the administration to prevent the worker from working for two consecutive shifts

Some hospitals prohibit us nurses from working a continuous 24-hour shift.

Everything within the framework of logic as well; when you make your plans, it must also be logical, otherwise the plan is meaningless, no matter how precise the theoretical conditions are.

Imagine if you said the price of a kilo of rice today is S, would the price of the total number of rice bags expected to be present in the entire land also be S...?

Not at all, of course. With the purchase of half of the world's rice, the price of the second half will gradually increase. Perhaps by the time you have bought three-quarters of the rice, the price per kilo of the last quarter will be four times... It is difficult, but it is a deep issue in economics. The more the demand increases and the supply decreases, the higher the price goes. Not to mention that it is legally not allowed because this will be a monopoly of goods for many governments, and the quantity you have will be reserved.

The matter here may be in hiring workers at market wages, but when you think of a huge number, you should expect the required wages to rise because the demand for workers has increased... Therefore, a project that is implemented in a year, if you try to implement it in four months, expect the wages to increase not only because the number of workers increases but also because for every hour of work, sometimes this is required. But remember the rule

A plan should be logical, and we will talk later about the algebraic values and sometimes not all the masses are equal to the sum and the rest in the section of the value...

Stagnation of plans

By stagnation of plans, I mean setting a plan that does not take into account changes and probabilities and its inability to change

Imagine if you were surprised one day in your life with an exam, a job interview, a trip, and more...

Therefore, remember what I told you that today must contain work of grade A and B to cancel it when needed

Stagnation of plans is one of the causes of failure because it is simply impossible to implement everything that is planned, and this is actually part of reality. You make a plan to buy iron from a factory, and then something happens and the factory stops, something goes wrong and the work stops, an unexpected exam happens tomorrow, and you are planning for the course

The detailed plan always includes alternative plans

One production line stops when the maintenance worker is present and the engineer is available in case of failure, and rest hours operate as needed.

Simply, when the manager decides not to make the work available to the person for 24 consecutive hours, even if an incident occurs, the person can continue after the 12-hour shift, but what if he has already worked a 24-hour shift here? It's difficult in the case of incorrect matters such as the absence of a colleague to continue the 24 hours after the 24.

Shortage of spare time.

What if the work is interrupted for hours due to power outages or if the internet is down or a worker is absent, or something happens and disrupts work according to the time frame.

Do you have any extra time to compensate for the error or the lack of time or the problem that occurred?

The contingency time is one of the most important things when working in groups and when your work is in an environment dependent on external factors, but even reading a book sometimes requires extra time.

Many times I have downloaded an online educational course and found a part or an external link to an important part that is not included in the course.

You assumed that the course or book took two or five hours, and then you were surprised to find that the course contains an important external part not included in the duration.

I do not mean by the pre -trial time that a worker in implementing something is more than required, but the backup time is essential for each point in the work to imagine if there is a mistake, delaying what or suggestion here, the backup time is valuable

To imagine that your day seemed and set a daily plan, do you need a backup time that is different because there is no need for a backup here. Every time is full of degree with a reserve time to work from the rest of the degrees and the time in business c and d is a backup time for business or b and all works can be It is a reserve time for the degree degree

But the most important here is that you have the option to postpone some of the work to tomorrow or after it, unlike the projects, so the absence of a precautionary time is disastrous because the plan is continuing for years

Chapter Six

This chapter discusses the reasons that lead you to failure that are related to the principles. The position of the same time, the distortion of its formulas, the absence of reviews of these principles, or rushing to establish them, and the double standards sometimes

The lack of principles

The lack of principles is one of the clear reasons for failure, but the most important thing is the distinction between principles and plans, so plans must be flexible and subject to change and sometimes articulated, but the principles are those fixed sentences that do not change, whatever and that is not that saying that the founder or thinker says and then goes on it but rather The list remains as long as the plan is present, the idea is under implementation and the project is on the job

Perhaps the principles sometimes arise on the strength of the vision of the place and its mission, or the knowledge of the person himself and his understanding of itself

Perhaps humanity takes truth, respect, and good character and clarity as its starting point.

And perhaps the institution takes justice, transparency, equality, governance, and community service as its principles...?

But whatever principles humanity sets for itself or the nation sets for itself in the form of a constitution or the company in the form of principles

they cannot be changed.

But here we are talking about the most dangerous reason for changing principles, which is the lack of them from the very beginning

Imagine if you are in your life and do not have principles to return to, how do you think...?

You might find yourself in a maze of work this year, trying to beautify your image in front of people, and then next year working to gather money even if it harms your appearance in front of people

So you might not have preserved your appearance nor gathered money

The principles alongside their organization to guide you in knowing yourself or in clarifying the institution's vision for its employees and customers also help both the individual and the institution from being merged into the community without a framework, vision, or clarity on the work and its judgments.

Companies that do not have declared principles may continue for short periods, but what happens after a change in the executive manager or a number of employees? How do the new ones follow the approach, ethics, and principles of the company that was set, and which were not set or even put into place verbally? Therefore, principles are the element that preserves for companies and individuals the origin of their methods and the fundamentals of their plans, the clarity of their vision, and the rules when changing plans, and the frameworks for work when there are differences and transparency when renewing...

Unclear principles

At times, there may be principles but they may not be clear enough to be implemented or not clear enough that everyone reads them with the meaning they understand. On the personal side, the lack of clarity in the principles may be a place for different interpretations according to each situation and each time the person returns to his principles.

Here is an example of clear principles

I am a Muslim person, following the Quran and the Sunnah of Prophet Muhammad to the best of my ability

Many may see principles as something unnecessary and postpone them until they forget and neglect them, and some may even believe that people do not need principles

But how do you plan and think without principles...?

When you plan and think and formulate ideas without principles, you might say "the end justifies the means." We will steal from the rich and give to the poor.

You formulate a plan on the backs of these families.

Yes, this might happen because you started thinking without having principles because there is nothing that prevents you from doing this.

But if you have principles of honesty in dealing, you will reject such ideas because they go against your principles...

What if a company or institution has no principles ...?

Here, when you start making plans, for example, if they have a goal to earn a certain amount this year, without principles, they might set up illegal plans for profit sometimes, or even plans that can help the company earn the amount this year without the ability to maintain success in the next year.

Without principles, a company can say that we will collect money from customers on the premise that we provide some benefit and then collect the money without providing the benefits. But strangely, the lack of clarity in principles can do the same thing. Imagine that the company puts justice in its principles, but without clarifying what justice is, with whom, and when ...?

Or quality does not know what quality, how, when, why, and who monitors it ...?

\nLack of principles is a cause of failure because you will not find boundaries that prevent you from forgetting something, but the lack of clarity in principles on the other hand may lead you to mistakenly think you are doing the right thing and achieving principles of justice, while due to its lack of clarity, you may find yourself infringing on the rights of others.\n

\nIf the principle of equality is not clear in the principles, perhaps a company that provides services to regular customers at the same level as advanced customers.\n

\nThe same applies to individuals and institutions alike.\n

\nUnlegitimacy of principles\n

Unconstitutionality of principles is one of the most obvious reasons for failure, unlike others, here the reason for failure is not the impact on performance or the inaccuracy of the plan, but simply because you place yourself under the jurisdiction of the law simply here, failure does not result from unclear or non-existent principles, or from any other reason, but because you have set principles that differ from the larger entity over you, which is the state or the institution that contains you.

Imagine if someone decided to establish a religious party in a civil state or a political party for men only, or if a company decided to impose a principle that prohibits women or followers of a certain religion or a certain group from working with it as a principle here, it would make the institution itself subject to law and prohibition, and sometimes it could lead to failure due to the bad reputation resulting from legal judgments against it, and even after changing the principles, the previous reputation remains attached to it.

But what about individuals? How can illegal principles be one of the reasons for failure?

Simply, whether the air of the individuals is the founders of that institution or part of it, or even if they only have personal principles that are hostile to the state, they place them under the jurisdiction of the law.

Therefore, all principles should fall under the framework of legality and legitimacy, otherwise they will be in a position that makes them fail judicially or legally.

Therefore, think about placing principles every time and make sure they flow with the largest institution or the highest authority.

Forgetting the principles

Imagine that you have provided everything you need from characteristics for you or the institution, then wrote them down in gold ink and put them in a file of values, closed it, and forgot about it.

What is its value ...?!

One of the reasons for the failure related to principles is not only the difference between them and the general characteristics of the principles, but sometimes it may be forgotten and neglected, or ignored, or perhaps you have set the principles but have not informed all the employees in the institution, or if you are an individual, you forgot the principles and neglected them and did not return to them...

The principles must be written and announced, and they must be referred to periodically or when decisions are made that will bring about a change, whether for you or for the institution. They must be clear and concise; you do not need a book of principles, perhaps 10 or 20 principles are sufficient, explained in sufficient detail for understanding, and announced on the website or listed in the printed copies of the guide or routine decisions so that no one is left out, and if possible, hang them in the offices...

As for the people, it is enough to add them to your daily planner or phone so that you can refer to them every time you start a decision or a new project or feel that you are failing and are not achieving what you hope for or that you are far from achieving your goals...

Why simply forgetting the principles is one of the causes of failure...?

Because forgetting the principles prevents the main goal from being achieved, and those principles were not written to fill empty spaces within a document or to complete a model for establishing an institution, but to be a law that governs all your thoughts and all the regulations and future plans of the institution

Abandoning the principles gradually

Unfortunately, sometimes or often, the process begins by looking at the principles and giving them their due value and position in the presentation and review before each meeting or before each crucial or non-crucial decision, and presenting them to all employees. Over time, the employees begin to change without presenting the principles to new employees, and after a period of time, the matter becomes forgotten. Sometimes, after setting the principles, people begin to implement them strictly and then start, for example, by being late hour by hour, and find themselves sleeping in the morning and waking up in the evening

Perhaps the company began with a principle of transparency, then started to delay presenting the plans to the employees, and then sectors of transparency were gradually eroded until the principle was eaten away and became just ink on paper.

Then if there are no sustainable and scheduled review plans to ensure that all decisions follow the established principles or to return to personal insight and reflect on the extent of adhering to his ideas and plans for his principles.

And if some negligence of the principles has been allowed, then he should review himself and understand the reason for this retreat.

Find yourself setting a principle in your life to review all your actions, and then after a period of time, it accumulates because you don't have time today to delay the review for tomorrow, and then you find that tomorrow has work to review and you forget about today and sometimes the week, and you start asking yourself, "Have I ever reviewed myself?" And every day, no real problem has occurred because gradualism is the greatest enemy of man. Perhaps you go through from black to white without understanding any of the dividing lines due to the presence of the gray in the middle, through which you find yourself gradually giving up the color you have set and the principle you have agreed with without realizing it.

Apply the principle of thrift in your life and do only what necessity dictates in spending or what benefits you in the long or short term.

Today you follow the film of a famous actor, and tomorrow you go to the cinema, which is just a form of self-indulgence, and gradually you find yourself spending in the presence of a musical event, which may lead to buying food for a general gathering or perhaps enough to buy a housing unit.

This matter will not appear as such and with such severity.

And so, with every step you take away from your principles, you repeat a well-known phrase, 'I've gone too far on this step,' until you find yourself completely distant from what you had set as principles.

Here, the gradual abandonment of principles is a cause of failure...

Situations of a single instance

One of the causes of failure that many people are unaware of is the situations of a single instance that those who do them think are just a slip that will not affect the principles that the person or institution has established for their work...

But what comes after this fleeting situation...?

What happens after you establish a principle and abandon it under the classification of a passing situation?

The act of abandoning principles for a single stance is akin to embezzling an amount of money and then investing in it.

What ...? Is this unacceptable ...?

This is what you do every time you abandon principles in a passing situation.

You think the situation will end peacefully and return to discipline and adherence to principles, but sometimes this situation is the bait for something bigger than giving up your principles and transitioning from committing to principles to randomness and non-commitment. When a person is stripped of their principles, they are like a moving object without a destination, even their own plans lack guidelines. Therefore, instead of their plan leading them to the fulfillment of their desires, they find themselves in a vicious cycle of repetition. You see situations that are fleeting, such as a conversation with a wild girl or injustice to someone you wouldn't repeat, or waking up late on a day to sell an illegal product in a pharmacy or having dinner with a friend without a plan.

On the other hand, the call to the girl won't end peacefully, and you'll find yourself needing to reconcile the next day and then calling the next day to end the communication. Or the illegal product has become evidence against you, either for not repeating the deal or because the friend you agreed to have dinner with has become evidence that you don't stick to the plan. And any refusal of a similar request will not be acceptable because you've done it before. Here, you enter the circle of failure through its widest doors, with a situation that you think is trivial.

The matter is exactly the same as giving up bad habits; it begins with a step and ends with a spectacular success. As soon as you give up one of your wrong principles or bad habits, it is as if you are transitioning from a cycle of failure to a cycle of success, on the broadest and most explicit level.

The cycle of failure here is failure, then frustration, and then remembering the failure, and frustration again.

The cycle of success, on the other hand, is success, then self-encouragement, and then another success. For example, by giving up self-criticism, such as "complaining about the reduction of yourself" when you fail, instead, you start with a clear plan and self-review, and find yourself succeeding.

There was one moment on the right path that moved you from the cycle of failure to the cycle of success.

I am also here repeating the same thing in case you are really doing a mistake for once, thinking it won't affect...

It will affect, and if it doesn't, it will put you in the next circle...

Distortion of Principles

Distortion of principles is one of the reasons for failure, whether for individuals or institutions, and here the failure is not due to the lack of principles, but sometimes due to the lack of belief in them, or not reviewing them, or not documenting them, and forgetting them, which leads to their distortion either intentionally or unintentionally...

Perhaps on a personal level, it is difficult to say that a person who sets principles for himself and then alters them is closer to foolishness than to anything else; I don't think the reader does that.

But here, principles are altered unintentionally due to the lack of documentation and neglect, just like anything that is neglected, such as setting the principle of commitment to your plans and then forgetting to look at the principles, only to find yourself wondering which plans did you commit to: were they the manager's plans at work or your own when the plans clash?

This may not begin with a complete reversal, but with just a simple alteration: I committed to a bedtime, and it became a matter of committing to a 6-hour bedtime, or as Hani Ramzi said, "Six - six and a half means..."

This is just a simple alteration and a slight neglect that leads to a gradual deviation; here, you are not altering the plan, but the principle upon which the plans originate.

But in institutions, the matter is different

Here, the distortion may be deliberate, driven by the desire of the parties involved to gain short-term benefits and forget about the greater impact...

You deal with a mobile company every day

What if the company decided to sell phantom charging cards, would anyone check behind it...?

Perhaps the matter is happening

But the most important thing is that when it does this, it loses its customer base and market confidence...

When two companies enter into a contract and set up a cooperation protocol or framework and then deviate from it slightly instead of adhering to its implementation at a specified time, they ignore a specified time because the time was not mentioned after the direct implementation was the norm...

Here, the most effective solutions to distortion of principles are clear wording, clarity of principles, and not leaving room for personal interpretations, which prevents distortion because here you, as a manager, may commit to implementing the matter based on your understanding because you are the one who set up the protocol, but the person who comes after you may not understand what you understood, and thus distort the principles unintentionally. This often happens in companies after the founders have passed away, and perhaps even with the intention of changing ethics...

Remember here that these principles are not set for a year or a decade, but they are originally set to endure even if they are reviewed; they are fundamentally meant to last long. You must write them with precision and ensure they are valid for comprehensive cases, not just for a specific amount but for a percentage, not for a person but for a status, so that it is not said that the Prophet passed away, who should we give our intelligence to...?

Remember whether you are working for yourself and setting principles, or if those principles are for a company, or if they are a cooperation protocol or a communication or a foundation creation rule. Clarity does not mean just that you understand it, but that everyone who reads it understands it. So that your death or livelihood is not one of the reasons for the failure of an institution or the collapse of the principles you set. They must be clear to the reader as it is said as if he will come from another planet...

Do not say 'he will understand...' Yes, he will understand, but through distortion and personal interpretation

Absence of Reviewing the Principles

These principles are created by humans, and a general principle is that any principle created by humans needs to be reviewed periodically. When we establish these principles, we have knowledge of a part of science, and over time, our knowledge of science or sciences increases, broadening our horizons with the increase of our experience or even the presence of issues arising from it or when you want to implement the principles. Although the presence of issues when applying the principles or even complaints about the inability to practically apply them are one of the most important reasons for reviewing the principles, these principles also need periodic reviews to remember what was established, whether personal or to ensure that everyone is committed to those principles if they are for an institution or a company or a collaboration protocol.

Why is the absence of review a cause for failure..?

Because simply, it means forgetting, distortion, or obsolescence as it is called.

For example, principles established for cooperation between two companies as a protocol cannot forget 10 years without review and then say it is valid for use. If it was truly valid, wouldn't everyone in both companies or two parties involved in the collaboration know about it?

Is it considered with due consideration in the current plans ..?

Is it still executable and clear to prevent any ambiguity from distortion or lack of understanding ..?

And is there a plan for periodic review of it ...?

I am not saying the duration because those principles are a state of the individual and differ from institutions..

But the most important thing is not to exceed the quarter..

But I won't give examples of not reviewing the principles because you have certainly fallen into the trap many times and you set plans that don't get implemented or goals that don't adhere to the intelligence of determination and realism and others..

But the most important thing is that knowing this reason leads you to remember the rule

The principle is set to be implemented then reviewed then implemented

There is no time to neglect or forget it, no time to ignore it, and no time for one-time standpoints..

The principle is a principle that is not distorted because it is clear..

Are your principles clear, reviewed, and remembered..?

And are they really defined and written down...?

And do you believe in it and adopt it just because others are practicing it...?

Here it will be executable

But it is also important to be right; here you are fulfilling the purpose for which it exists, which is life as you love to live it, and not falling into a cycle of failure.

Being hasty in adopting principles

One of the reasons for failure for institutions is to rush to set the principles. These principles are not placed for application in a time or circumstances, but rather a constitution based on a large time period and may not change and change them. A lot of trouble will require the foundations of the building. Sirte, you are not able to change it, nor are you able to continue in the application

And rushing in the development of personal principles may be mostly due to lack of understanding or self -confidence.

Perhaps the lack of knowledge of local or international legal rules in the field, especially when moving from country to country

Often, the countries set special conditions, laws and policies that differ from others, and when you move on your work to them, you adhere to these laws. Language and cultural understanding and perhaps in appreciation of the facts of facts that may be a history of the past in less than an hour, what about this principle in the agreement that determines a person or a place for the meeting and takes opinion. jealousy

The hurry here blinds the person or the institution from seeing the expected or even unexpected changes, and sometimes not only this, but also in documenting agreements or proportions or their calculation, these principles are like the knife tied to the neck: moving it kills and leaving it causes pain.

hurrying to establish principles can also work like working without a plan, falling into repetitive cycles of errors. One of the axioms that I don't think anyone would dispute is learning from past mistakes.

Double standards

One of the famous reasons for failure, even up to covering the media, is the multiplicity of principles for the same purpose. Even though it may seem logical that each position has its own argument and each person has their own capacity, and that we should determine each person or entity with whom we deal in a special way, the funny thing is that humor is not part of the principles. A principle like honesty cannot be said, for example, honesty respects the family and relatives and trades with others, because the majority of traders do this.

Your principles are your principles that are indivisible, otherwise your gain from violating the principles in something will be a loss on the other hand. About a good reputation, you think it is a close gain, I am with you, but the longest side is a loss

The principles are not only to deal with people. If your lack of respect for your principles and their unification in dealing with companies is lost by customers 'confidence, what about your personal principles .....

There is no doubt that you permeate it or its multiplicity, and you may say to yourself, "No, it is the day of the vacation, we do not have to wake up early."

Or, "No, it is a defensive work and everything is permissible" nothing without successful principles, as well as the double standards and principles, if you or even as a company when it determines the principles of quality and then allows a product less than what is committed to its standards of quality. There is no doubt that it carries the name of the company and its slogan, and here the customer will not say it is a less Survival, but the rest of the company's products are still good

It turns into a part of the company's reputation and nature of work that such a company allows this level of quality, which contradicts its fundamental principles.

Chapter Seven

This chapter discusses the reasons for failure related to the reputation of the institution or the individual. Here we mention six reasons, including the absence of knowledge initially, a bad reputation, the peacock reputation, exaggerated reputation, trendy reputation, and spectacular failure in reputation.

Ignorance itself

I mean here not being known by people for you or the institution, and this may be a cause of failure for the institution because people do not trust those they do not know and may not even think of dealing with you here not because you are bad but because you are unknown. Knowledge here may come through an advertisement for a new product from a previously known company or a new announcement for a new company, or sometimes through an advertisement for a film or service or others. What matters is that the institution introduces itself.

Here, my study on digital marketing reminds me of the stages of advertising, which are three:

The first is brand identity advertising, which is an advertising purpose to make people aware that you exist. Through brand identity advertising, people get to know your services, often in a pleasant way, such as distributing printed gifts or the like. Perhaps one of the company's consultants and experts provides an educational session for people, then introduces them to the company. The third is decision-making advertising, which involves advertising a product and then providing a way to purchase or make direct contact.

Here, it is often the case that people move from the stage of not knowing you to the stage of knowing how to contact you, but the whole point is that you make people aware that you exist as an institution and that you provide services, and that they can contact you in some way. Perhaps I am not available to link specific advertising ideas to the advertising of a product, such as thirst in Pepsi ads and celebrities in advertisements. But the key point here is to make people know you and your services and how they can communicate with you.

Or if you are an individual and not an institution, the matter is different. Although both cases should be preceded by a stage of self-awareness for the individual and the vision for the institution, the most important for the individual here is to start building good relationships and communicating with everyone related to their work and how they can serve them. The absence of knowledge is a cause of failure because simply no one knows you from the beginning to communicate with you or support you or help you or advise you. No one knows what you need to provide you with services. This certainly will not happen before you understand yourself. The clearer you are in defining yourself, the easier it is for people to recognize you.

Bad Reputation

In the previous part, the problem was a lack of knowledge, but it was not dangerous because you started from zero. But here, the real problem is starting from below zero; you are known, and you have a bad reputation. Starting here is harder than starting first time because simply, you have haters and those who speak ill of your reputation. These are previous clients of yours as an institution, and they do not trust you. These clients not only have their own opinions but in hours, their opinions might turn into public opinion. We live in the age of social media, where opinions are shared, and now opinions are even sold. Perhaps no one will buy from someone who supports and flatters you, but when it comes to reputation, remember that an unsatisfied customer can turn into a crowd of imaginary unsatisfied customers. Perhaps, by luck, this might cost you a little, but dear, if you manage a company or an institution, every unsatisfied customer increases the chance of general dissatisfaction through buying opinions on social media or even through free tools, and it might lead you to consumer protection lawsuits and various issues. All this starts with an unsatisfied customer about the company or delayed service delivery or something else. But what about the transfer between people and customer complaints to each other?

Unfortunately, some are affected by the trend and many can defend and share experiences they have not undergone, not out of necessity but out of respect, because this client has been humiliated and attacked and has lost his right, and how many supporters?

The matter differs when we mention individuals, as institutions may deal with larger numbers, therefore the likelihood of tarnishing the reputation is greater than that of individuals whose reputation may be tarnished due to unsatisfactory dealings with a friend or even a colleague who spreads a bad or incorrect idea.

But how does this lead to failure...?

For the institution, a bad reputation prevents customers and potential customers from dealing with you, thus a decrease in the services provided, and sometimes it reaches the extent of boycott or even general dissatisfaction, and it may be a legal issue and billions in damages. The matter may be similar partially in individuals, but what adds to it is that a bad reputation can also turn into a discouraging aspect for your close friends or even your own perspective of yourself due to the reviews and advice you receive with the bad reputation, not to mention the lower job offers and more...

Turkey's reputation

That reputation of the turkey is a strange but realistic theory

It may not be a direct cause of failure, but it can lead to it in many cases, both in companies and individuals, even to clarify this term for the first time, I mention it, but what is the meaning of the reputation of the turkey this ..?

Simply imagine yourself walking down a street in a poor area as a simple person and encountering a shop that looks very grand, next to another one that looks simple and has a vending machine for selling recharge cards and chargers and other things, and you want to buy a recharge card

Are you going to the small place or the luxurious place...?

Most of what I've seen and dealt with is the small place because it doesn't expect the luxurious place to provide the service of shipping cards. Perhaps it looks like an agency for mobile companies and perhaps the name is in English. Even if it is in Arabic, many do not know how to read, and most of those who can read do not read the truth.

I may differ from you in opinion.

Let's try another example about that girl who studies medicine and publishes that she has rejected people from the medical college, engineers, and many who are of status and position.

Would you apply for a simple job...?

Of course, you wouldn't...

Would someone studying medicine apply for it? Of course not, as she has rejected many, turning her reputation into this person, not the bad one, but the good one who wouldn't accept people like us, I mean the writer...

Simply, if you're unemployed and you publish on your LinkedIn profile that you work at a company, will anyone contact you to offer a job, even if it's just your neighbors supporting you...?

Of course, no one thinks you're actually working hard ...!

Imagine a company offering a magnificent product that looks elegant on the shelf but no one knows about it and it seems expensive

How many people would refuse to put it in their shopping cart out of fear of the price..

Simply put, the concept of the peacock's reputation is that people refuse to deal with a person, company, service, or product because they believe it is more expensive and of greater value than expected

Exaggerated Reputation

The concept of exaggerated reputation is that you offer a certain service or product with specific characteristics, and while advertising it, you raise the expectations of the buyers more than necessary. For example, a product that treats dandruff or at least helps with it for 10 uses, and you advertise that it does so in just one use; this is what is called exaggerated reputation. Imagine if you offer independent services and say that you execute large projects and perform wonders in your services, and when someone asks you based on this exaggerated reputation, I wouldn't say you would find a bad outcome, but at least you would find yourself at a level that does not match what you say in executing the services. This is what is called exaggerated reputation.

Perhaps the other issue under the same title is those who say they offer free courses, then they talk to you about administrative fees or say that the service price is X for the first month, and then you find out that the price is four or five times that after that.

Very simply, exaggerated reputation leads to failure first because you claim to do or provide more than reality, and secondly, you may deceive the customer, causing them to lose trust in you or raise their expectations of you. If you say you are proficient in a language or programming language, and the interlocutor starts asking advanced questions and you fail, perhaps if you said you were a beginner, they would ask questions you understand, and he needs someone who is a beginner. But by deceiving him and raising the ceiling of his expectations, then you meet him with the first question...On a personal level, sometimes the matter is related to false self-confidence. Instead of realizing that your level in a certain skill is a beginner and you need training and education at this level, instead, you convince yourself and those around you that you are at a higher level. Here, you do not benefit from their advanced talk, nor do they trust you. Every time you are asked to perform a task that you fail at, you turn from a successful person to a failure. The beginner learns and grows, but the person who is falsely confident does not do so, and may even turn the person in front of him from advice to fear because he thinks you know more than him, and therefore how can he advise you...?

The trend's reputation "appears for a short and quick period then returns"

The trend's reputation may be based on the previous stage, simply in the beginning, no one knows you, then people start to know you, and your reputation gradually increases. This is a natural occurrence, whether for companies or individuals

But sometimes, overnight, a person goes from being unknown to known, and an unknown institution becomes famous. Perhaps both had limited knowledge, but what is strange is the speed of the transformation in the spread of their knowledge

The secret of social media, my friend

You will find a famous person hitting someone

or a company inviting the president or king of the country for the opening, or a company distributing millions to customers for free, or one of the celebrities showing the ad to them

The matter is simply called a trend

But the concept of a trend today has become more known and famous

But why is the trend's reputation one of the reasons for failure...?

Simply because it is often built without a plan, but the planned trend is something else, a successful advertising style. But here you find the person has become famous without a plan and then forgets without a plan. The strange thing is that sometimes the sudden increase in demand for the product can be a reason for failure. Imagine you are providing a service to execute something within a company of 4 employees, and then after the trend, the demand increased by 600%. Can you handle it?

There are possibilities, the first being that you rush the services and reduce the quality, which will harm your reputation in the long run, or you decide to delay, and here you also harm your reputation. Moreover, trends often find opposition campaigns for the sake of opposition, just to insult you, not because of experience, but just for the sake of opposition. This may be due to the trend going beyond the acceptable limit.

There are many scenarios where the trend's reputation turns into a reason for failure unless the trend is meticulously planned. Here, it is not a trend but a known advertising style, like those companies that create problems before releasing a new book to increase demand for it or create a specific scene at a place to increase demand. All this is advertising thinking, even some use anonymous advertising styles to increase questions about the product or service or even to enter the trend to advertise their products. Social media helps with this, but even creating a trend as advertising can be a reason for failure because it costs a lot to know the temporary service or person, and then when the person stops paying, this costs a lot over time and has less impact or it stops the trend, and here the matter turns into a quick failure in reputation.

Failure of the notorious reputation

Failure of the notorious reputation is one of the reasons resulting from not evaluating the situation in disaster cases and sometimes negligence

Imagine if an airport company's website suddenly stops working and communication is interrupted for two days....!

Imagine if a person whose reputation is known is subjected to a cyber attack that destroys all communication profiles with them ...!

Imagine if a sheikh or an ascetic or a devotee in a religion appeared in an unseemly scene or if a company's shares collapsed in the stock market ...?

The abysmal failure can be represented as a general failure without prior warning.

Therefore, the abysmal failure in reputation is the sudden fall of reputation for a person or place due to artificial motives or calamities, sometimes, but it may also be due to a poor assessment of situations and accumulations. Imagine finding a place that leaks gas or water, broken, and trying to glue it with adhesive ...?

Or that the place you are in is about to collapse, but you are decorating its walls with wood to hide the cracks in the walls or that you are burdened with loans and can only pay off with new loans.

Here, at some point, things reach a point where they can no longer wait, as the cracks have reached their limit and the loans have reached their limit of interest, and the concealment of your hatred from people has caused a stir.

Then, suddenly, the matter turns into an explosion, like this cylinder filled with gas, and with a certain amount of pressure without prior warning, it explodes.

Then you find no gas, no cylinder, and not even the place, except after the fire has been lit for hours.

Imagine through social media that everyone has problems with you, but no one knows this. Suddenly, a girl starts talking about her problem, and suddenly the muted, sincere, and false voices come out, and the matter turns from a trend in your favor to a trend against you...

Or even imagine what you mentioned in the opposing campaigns in trend cases...

Imagine that people have become accustomed to buying from you for a specific product, and then one day, there was a poisoning incident due to your product, or a case was filed against you that gained media momentum and was won against you here, this is where the absurd failure in reputation occurs...

Therefore, you must always review and evaluate, and deal with complaints seriously, and even before complaints, take random samples seriously and deal strictly with mistakes and shortcomings, as your reputation may be at stake at any moment without prior warning...

Chapter Eight

This chapter discusses the causes of failure associated with opportunities, and we mention fourteen because

the meaning of crossing the river and adapting, the narrow perspective and the perspective of diversity, the penal conditions and the added quality

the misunderstanding of opportunities

One of the most related terms to success is opportunities, therefore, it is easy to consider the misunderstanding of the term "opportunities" as one of the reasons for failure

What are opportunities if ...?

The opportunities are the material things or services that are available at less than their value or even at a fair investment value in some cases

When you need a pair of shoes and find one at a fair price, it might seem like this

What is the opportunity in this ..?!

But how many times can you be deceived and buy it even at 110 percent of its actual price ..?

This may seem strange because the price of the shoe may not make a difference, but for example, buying a house at a fair price is not an ordinary thing because the purchase process is usually carried out through what is called a broker here. If the seller offers the house at a fair price, it is natural that you would pay more than the fair price because you are also paying a part to the broker as well...

But since you found the opportunity to buy directly from the property owner, that is an opportunity

So our wrong understanding of the opportunity is that it is a gold hanging on a silver plate with a big piece of meat for free

That is not true, but there is a danger in this wrong understanding of opportunities. Seeing the opportunity as in the previous example, a gold hanging and a silver plate, may sometimes make you a victim of some swindlers...

Opportunities are the tangible and intangible things and services available at a fair price, sometimes even less than fair, and rarely much less than fair.

But free opportunities are never available...

As some say in military thinking, "If you see the path clear of obstacles, know that it is a trap ...!"

It is not logical to find free opportunities now. This is not a threat but a warning.

When I say "free," I'm not talking about messages like "Congratulations, you've earned 500 pounds" on some internet blog because maybe the reader of this book isn't that stupid, but about those offers that come here and there every day, "Charge and earn 1000 pounds" or others, or even "Enter your information and you'll get a recognized course from the Ministry of Foreign Affairs "

Although I don't understand the meaning of a course being recognized by the Foreign Ministry or its actual recognition, but even the idea of a free opportunity is strange

I followed up on some opportunities and found that they said "The opportunity is free and the certificate is 2500 pounds..." It's not free if it's just a way to advertise and attract attention

And even other opportunities that were followed up on, most of them didn't offer services at all; they were just collecting your data... I came across a day when perhaps some of you also saw a company offering thousands and millions of user numbers in Excel files as a way to start promotional advertising services

Said to myself, "How can these companies have such huge amounts of data and phone numbers" and remembered that I just registered my data with one of the companies to get a free English language course...

Here I am not talking about the fact that all opportunities are like this...

But the majority is because it is difficult to understand the logic of free services at that time, which is just a business if...

Ignore the opportunities

This part may seem contradictory to the chapter's introduction, as ignoring opportunities is one of the causes of failure, and the introduction fears me from the fear of opportunities in this way...?

The answer lies in the true understanding of opportunities

When I tell you that there are false opportunities and that opportunities are often of fair value and not the cheapest, I tell you that those fair opportunities are opportunities and those opportunities at a lower price than fair are opportunities, but with taking caution with them

Ignoring opportunities is not one of the causes of failure not because you lose the value of the opportunity but because you regret after losing the opportunity

Which one is preferable, whether it is a chance or not ..?

Although this is difficult, the first option is to avoid risk

I am not saying that success is fundamentally free from risk, and failure is risk, but this is only when the two sides are equal ..

The matter may not be clear

The opportunities give us a strong push towards achieving what we want, but they are often elusive and not obvious to the general public, unless people rush to seize them, and it won't be here as an opportunity.

Therefore, from the perspective of the majority, the opportunity is not an opportunity, and only those who understand the meaning of an opportunity will find it and notice it...

But for those who do not know its meaning, either they will not find the opportunity or they will search for it and be exploited by false opportunities.

So ignoring opportunities may be due to ignorance of them and also due to not understanding your goals from the very beginning;

what do you want...? What serves this against a reasonable opportunity is an opportunity.

Ignoring opportunities can sometimes be waiting for a golden ticket or what some call the idealism.

Perhaps you are working on a project and waiting for the moment that your project is complete without any mistakes to hand it over, and this will not happen. Or you may be waiting for someone to offer you a free service, and this will not happen. But the problem of not having an opportunity is much better than the deceit and false opportunities we talk about after this.

The most important thing is to know the opportunity well and take advantage of it as soon as you find it.

What is an opportunity? It is a value that you need at a fair price or a value that you own until...

Illusory Opportunities

You might think I'm talking about the same idea, and you're right

Understanding opportunities prevents you from ignoring opportunities or falling into the illusion of opportunities

The matter is simple; it is a process of balance between the nature of real opportunities and the illusion of opportunities

Illusory opportunities are those that do not serve your goals...

Your definition of this prevents you from much chatter...

Because you might see something that people are rushing to...

Perhaps a beautiful girl everyone is pursuing and she rejects, and you think she is accepting you, or a commodity that is told to you is the last piece...

You are not in competition with anyone

The real opportunity serves your interests, so if everyone sees it as beneficial, this will not affect it being an opportunity for you

Unless you intend to sell it

But this is originally if it can be sold, for example, the beautiful girl who might accept you after rejecting a hundred young men might not serve your vision of marriage for stability, few problems, and misunderstandings, and she might be a curse rather than an opportunity

Occasionally, you enter the supermarket looking for a bag of bread and find three for the price of two; you want one.

So you buy the second one hoping for the third.

It's just an illusion of an opportunity for you because you don't want the third and the second.

There are many illusions of opportunities that provide a market evaluation for them.

It should be reminded here that all voices can be bought, so the product that is said to be valuable online and has been sold 500 million of it does not mean that it is good, but it may mean that the company has spent a lot on advertising, and as a buyer, you will pay for the product and the cost of marketing...

This is if it is a false opportunity of the good type, yes, because some false opportunities may be paying money for nothing...

I heard about what is called "relaxers"...

or "fraudsters in Egypt"...

These people who claim to be collecting money for investment then generously pay a substantial fee to some for the first month, and here the participation in the folly begins to spread the idea. People start paying money, and suddenly, after the person has collected millions, they begin to pay a simple share as a monthly fee for some.

The person disappears.

Perhaps they are found or not, but the idea of the illusionary opportunities still exists.

And although some learn from their mistakes, they still fall into the same illusionary opportunities again and again as long as they do not know the concept of opportunities and even look at real opportunities as not being opportunities because they do not satisfy their greed.

greed

greed, as one of the causes of failure, lies in a person's desire to gain a lot and their longing for more. It may seem instinctive in a person, but the greed here that the human being loves to be better is not greed but ambition.

But greed, as one of the causes of failure, is simply ignorance; it is the human will to achieve more profit than expected without exerting more effort than expected, and the result is an unexpected loss.

So the person who is offered to pay an amount and receive more monthly money than the bank's interest or the reasonable gain, is greedy because he wants to achieve more money without effort, and this idea is good, but when you sit down and think and put an idea for the project and stay up at night and lose and learn and gain...

But the idea of making a big profit just because you put money with someone else was initially for that person to take this person's money from the bank and repay it with lower interest than what it does with people as it promises them.

This is not logical and I repeat, the opportunity is not hanging by a thread; it is not gold or silver but just a fair price for the value...

The other and bad thing about greed as one of the causes of failure is that the person who is greedy is not cooperative; he does not like to make profits together "I win alone or we don't win." This is called in management science "Non-cooperative thinking."

And thus, it causes failure because in solving problems, it often moves away from understanding only "I win" and creates conflicts, especially with people of the same mindset...

The previous discussion might seem like a recipe for failure for institutions as a result of greed, but for individuals as well, merely having the will to achieve great success without working leads to failure because you do not consider the logical steps but put your money in illusory opportunities, hoping to earn more without thinking.

Unfortunately, there are many who exploit this mindset and start to prey on it as in the following section.

The Trap

Due to the ignorance of some, the greed of others, and perhaps the neglect of many to the concept of opportunities.

Many take advantage of this opportunity to make profits through the foolishness of others, known as the trap. Imagine with me the image of a fox looking at a piece of bread with joy and saying to himself, "Good food," and forgetting to look at the fishing tool it contains that will take him and that morsel to hell...

The illusion of opportunities may be one form of the trap.

But the trap sometimes includes lavish advertisements and satisfied customer opinions and maybe even persuasive methods...

With a little understanding of a person's goal and principles and a little greed, the person becomes an easy prey for fraud and deception and theft. This is certainly a form of failure for individuals, but even institutions cannot escape this unless they tear themselves apart. The pitfalls for institutions are also there. Some institutions offer generous offers to the others to sign cooperation protocols, and with the generous offer, the other one ignores the review of the large terms in return...

The idea of the trap is simply to blind a person to the counterpart they are driven by and the lost value they pay for, while highlighting what they gain...

It may be one use of the trap to catch those people involved in drug trafficking or murderers, but it is also used criminally against both the good and the foolish alike...

Therefore, I bring you back to the first chapter and ask you what is your goal? What do you want? And what is your plan to achieve this...? What are your principles and add what are your expectations and understanding of life...

If some soldiers say "A path without obstacles is a sign of a trap," I say to you, "Perhaps, although it is rare, there are some paths without obstacles in civilian life, but the most important thing is to think clearly about logic and look around to take your precautions and not ignore the natural opportunities that come with fair prices in pursuit of golden opportunities and free services..."

Nothing is free ..

One of my friends used to say to me, "If you don't pay for the item, know that you are the item."

Reliance on a single point

One of the reasons for failure related to the concept of opportunities is reliance on a single point ..

You might hear that the price of the dollar, gold, or something else is falling and suddenly, you want to buy everything you have... and its price crashes.

Maybe you rely on your friend for everything, and suddenly they die or leave you.

Reliance on a single point for individuals, institutions, and others is one of the causes of failure based on opportunity estimates...

You may have heard from me before that evaluation depends on sustainability.

If you rely on one company, then the likelihood of your downfall, if it happens, is close to one. But if you rely on 5 companies, then the likelihood of your downfall, if it happens, is reduced to the product of the fractions of their failure rates, which is much lower.

One day, I opened my phone to browse a file using a text reading program and it froze... And because I relied on it alone, it caused me a problem. Since that incident, I use three or four programs alternately...

The matter may be natural and sometimes deliberate as a kind of trap...

Some technology companies now offer their smart services for free without any conditions and pay a lot for this. So when everyone started to rely on them, they began to impose conditions and you are forced to use them.

Perhaps you also don't feel those conditions because those companies use a gradual approach to changes; they start by reducing free services and offering paid ones...

Another application of this is the backup we use even if the sites collapse; we use those backups...

Maybe you are accustomed in my field of study to the double-checking review because there is no way to know the patient from their name and medical number, as the name may be similar and the number may be misread...

The matter may seem simple, but sometimes we may use a value against not relying on a single point, and perhaps the preferred program you use may need to use one less preferably and with more features...

an artificial intelligence tool that creates something for you, you need 5 or even 10 tools, or even to download some of them to work in an offline mode

to work with what you are working with, you need to do some side work in case your manager ends your services

the matter may be a waste of effort, but it is a safeguard

like the insurance this man has when he stands on the ladder and holds the rope

Maybe this rope bothers him, but it will be the lifeline

And although this lifeline may not be used very often, you might need it

It's strange that some people just make plans for redundancy in dependability and don't use or test them

And that's a disaster because if you need this and it doesn't work, despite having paid a lot for it

The person who works in one field and learns another but does not try working with it a little during his work, will not be able to work in the other field...

The matter may be in simple things like the belt of the pants if one of the buttons breaks or even a water bottle if it breaks, but it may extend to the pluralism in international relations and business relations and what is greater than this...

Just understand why relying on one point is one of the reasons for failure...

Because it makes your fall dependent on the fall of the point, and the more points there are, the lower the rate of falling. But also beware of excessive multiplicity; you may need three or four points but not a hundred, as this will increase the burdens and the lost values and the poor storage of value.

Fear of risk

The idea that any opportunity in the world will have a very difficult part of the risk

Because you are simply trying a new need and a new way, and no one knows it before you, or at least you are not aware of it.

But as follows in fear of risk, this is one of the reasons for the failure associated with opportunities

For example, if we say that the value of gold is fixed and you won't lose, and the value of the products you will buy to sell may decrease due to poor storage or even expiration because you didn't send them...

So the fear of risk is saying why try something and lose, let me stay safe and without taking any risk...

Simply this leads to you avoiding any profit... because you are afraid of the loss...

Well, isn't loss possible in risk...?

Maybe possible, but as long as I am aware of the problems that might confront me, the risk factor decreases because you will be aware of where the problems are coming from and will avoid them

It's possible, but you avoid it...

But avoid the risk and the gain will ultimately be a stable point for you in a developing world; it is not enough to maintain your status, but to move forward

There is risk... but there is gain

Avoid the risk factor, the one that decides on slow death in the desert due to getting lost

Instead of seeking water or food, or finding a path to survival and spreading distress messages or doing anything else

No...he decides not to take any risks and he continues in peace

He will conserve his energy, but over time, he will lose his ability to take risks altogether

Because his energy is not exhausted to allow him to do so

The risk is one of the fundamental principles of trade and through it, growth is achieved, but when it is based on expectations and market study and in life in general, risk becomes essential for growth, whether in the form of experiments or even in the form of mistakes and learning from them

Without risk, we would not have discovered all the medicines given in hospitals ..

And although risk sometimes has heavy consequences - no one denies it - but with precise calculations, it can be just a successful logical step ..

Therefore, the solution is to think about what we want, what our plan is, what opportunities are in front of us, and also what the risks are. Sometimes we need to analyze risks for companies, for example, semi-annually, which is a well-known analysis in business management. But even in personal decisions where there is a risk, you need to ponder and calculate the gains and losses, the advantages and disadvantages, and understand the disadvantages not only to show them to you but also to give you the ability to overcome them...

Waiting

Waiting is the greatest enemy of man in my view and not just the cause of failure. Although sometimes precise calculations are required, just thinking about waiting is a terrifying thing, and I'm not talking about those times when you start the pre-execution procedures, but rather about the period when you wait for a change in your surrounding circumstances or for someone to take a certain action to give you a response... It is truly exhausting because you do not know when this will happen, if it will happen, and what the consequences will be...

It is as if someone says, 'I am building a building, and we will not wait until the price of iron falls' or something like that, or that you go to a meeting with someone scheduled for 7:30 and you wait until 9.

Because simply while waiting, you are wasting time and saying the curve is approaching, yes the price of iron is falling then rising, or if your friend didn't come on time and you waited for an hour, you probably say he won't wait any longer...

Simply if you forget the principles you set for yourself, maybe one of them was not to gradually accept deviation from appointments...

The matter is like a desperate attempt to adapt...

In one of the experiments I conducted on a frog, it adapted to the heat until the point where it no longer lived because the temperature reached the deadly degree...

You are waiting for a better opportunity than the current one and forget that having something available at a fair value in itself is enough of an opportunity

Perhaps because you have made a mistake in the equation because you simply, for example, might say the phone costs so much and I am waiting for it to reach a price like this

First, if the price is appropriate, then it is an opportunity and get it even if the price goes down in the future because you did not lose anything because it is a product for use, not for sale, and therefore the time you save for using it is enough so that you do not have to pay more

But the matter is different when it comes to buying materials for sale, perhaps sometimes you wait for a good opportunity

But it is a fact that you should not wait as long as the opportunity is in front of you and you understand the meaning of that word well

Viewpoint of crossing the river

The viewpoint of crossing the river is one of the strange ideas when discussing it as one of the causes of failure

Most people only think about the bright side of the procedure, and what they look at is crossing the river

But what comes after crossing the river?

What about the other rivers, mountains, plateaus, and swamps?

What's beyond the river...?

The idea itself is silly.

When you look at it

As long as you cross the river and do something difficult, then if I succeed ..

Maybe the idea of achieving what you want is tiring, but it doesn't mean that being tired means achieving what you want

Many here look on, and the bitterness of the medicine is proportionate to its effectiveness, and the effort is proportionate to what is achieved .. And this is strange and foolish again

crossing the river and your effort does not guarantee that you will reach it; perhaps crossing the river is part of the plan, but in itself, it is no more than an adventure...

Exploration in itself is one of the important things, but when it has a goal and a plan and safety measures...

But the perspective of crossing the river here is the view of people seeing difficulties as the path to success...

This may be related to your understanding of your goal and your definition of opportunities in the basics; in essence, opportunity means something or a service with fair value...

It also should not be more than its value...

When you create a medicine that treats the heart but destroys the kidney, this is not an achievement...

And when you cross the river to reach a place safer from predators, do not forget also that you are far from food...

Although environmental problems often require caution and change, change requires a plan so that you do not move from bad to worse. With your decision to cross the river, leave the company, or even end your relationship or divorce, or change your home, you may get rid of some of the problems you have, but wisdom lies in balancing both sides, between where you are and where you are going, in search of the best place, ignoring that every place has its own problems...

Listen often to someone who works in a field that others envy for what they achieve and forget that when they entered their field, they envied themselves for what they achieved within it

Now, here they are, blaming themselves...

Sometimes, things that are far away seem beautiful because you see them only from the outside, and perhaps that is a trick, as most poisonous animals are colorful and look beautiful, while what can be eaten is usually without any distinctive color

Perhaps the idea is often actually...

You see the other side of the river and the other company as paradise, but you don't know what's going on behind the scenes...

Therefore, whether you are an individual or an institution, before changing reality, think twice about the good things you have and once about the negative aspects of the place you are moving to or the situation you are transitioning to...

And I am sure you will also think concurrently about the problems you have and the benefits there... Now, by balancing the four aspects, the idea of updating and crossing the river, as we call it here, turns into a better state... Even if those thoughts don't stop you from changing, which is certainly not the goal, because the basic goal is to achieve what we want...

At least, it will give you an understanding and anticipation of the expected problems to solve them in advance...

Adaptation

On the contrary to the previous perspective, crossing the river and the current situation being worse than if we had moved or changed, here adaptation is one of the reasons for failure in the long term...

Adaptation in its simple meaning is not a cause of failure, but long-term adaptation is a cause of failure...

When you decide to work in a company based on experience, skills, and capabilities, of course, you may have other opportunities...

Maybe you're capable of programming websites or diagnosing diseases, but this certainly doesn't negate the fact that you can't necessarily move two papers from one office to another or post a content on social media pages...

Therefore, your work as a programmer may require you to post content on social media and as a doctor to move two papers from one office to another containing the patient's diagnosis...

But what about ...?

What if your job is originally as a trainee under another web developer or as an assistant doctor...

Did you find yourself constantly engaging in social media or shifting papers...?

Here is the concept of adaptation, which is one of the reasons for failure...

Adaptation, if it is one of the reasons for failure, is the transition from the basic skills and capabilities you learned to work with to the lateral skills you can do, but many do them just like you...

Can you ask a question here...?

What is the problem if I am described as a doctor and only do this or as a nurse and I only transfer blood samples or as a web developer and I only publish articles...

The problem does not lie in the short term, my dear, as long as you work in that company or clinic, you will earn what you earn, whether as a doctor diagnosing diseases or a doctor transferring papers...

The problem, my friend, lies in maintaining your skills and knowledge and developing yourself...

> You are adapting to a daily routine that does not suit you, ignoring what suits you in essence. Over time, you will become just a carrier of papers, a poster publisher, and a sample connector. You will not be able to do anything else, and with time, you will turn from a doctor with experience working in any hospital to just a doctor who does not know how to practice medicine, and in doing so, his work will be tied to the place as being a doctor. If he is expelled, he will no longer be a doctor or a web developer or even a nurse...
>
> Here you are defining yourself and gradually transforming yourself from yourself to just a cog in a huge machine, even though this is not your job ..
>
> But the problem lies in the state when you move from place to place or are expelled ..
>
> Because you have turned from a professional to an employee

Because you simply turned from a man who earns a living from knowledge he has and relies on God to just a person who does what is requested of him ..

Maybe adaptation in the eyes of some means flexibility, but that flexibility is not a cause of failure in itself as long as it has not led to shortcomings in other matters...

But here, adaptation as one of the causes of failure is a lifestyle that turns you from a free person into a slave and from a professional who works anywhere into an employee who does not know how long he will keep this job...

Narrow-mindedness

One of the causes of failure for both individuals and institutions is narrow-mindedness... It simply means looking at a little around you without taking a step back to get a comprehensive view of the entire picture...

Limiting perspective can be part of failure during the stage of self-definition, or even during the productive stage.

The person begins to scrutinize and focus on the details of the small parts and forgets the complete picture.

He sees a small drop in price amidst declines that are as trivial as sawdust and forgets a series of prolonged increases that lasted for years.

Limiting perspective here leads to failure not because you see this decline, but because by focusing on this small decline, you distract yourself from the larger problem.

One of the greatest examples of this may be the comfort of a patient with small foot clots at the moment of their transition and before they reach the lungs.

At times, a narrow perspective in looking at a problem to solve it prevents reaching a real solution, and all it does is lead to a false solution...

One of the speakers was saying to us, "What if I told you how to enter a villa for this room...?"

And here everyone began to think...

This is my point, or I break the door, or I trick the elephant, or ... or ... and so on

But this is just a narrow perspective ..

You look at the problem and forget to understand the cause of it ..

If the required is to let the elephant enter the room

What is the purpose of coming up here ...?

It is not futile; it is the basis of the solution because if the elephant has five solutions, perhaps there are fifty solutions to the fundamental problem that we need for the elephant to enter the room...

Conventional problem-solving skills are part of narrow-mindedness

When you look at this driver and say that he is speeding...

And start thinking about tools to reduce speed as if you have identified the primary problem as being speed

This is a narrow perspective

Because speed in itself is not the primary problem, perhaps the injuries in accidents

If we consider speed to be the problem

We installed the radars and monitored the speed

But when we look at the broader perspective

at the problem of accidents and fatalities from it

we may think of traffic intersections, wide roads, good lighting, and safe crossings for people

Instead of the foolish ways in bumps and radars and traffic signals ..

Ignorance of the perspective of pluralism

Our differences on the planet and in the universe are a great blessing, as it is said, "If it were not for the differences in tastes, there would be no market for goods." Similarly, in this difference, our opinions about something may be different here, the matter begins to seem very strange, but in reality, it is simpler than it seems

One of the jurisconsults might say, 'Let us look at the opinion of others, and if it is right and convincing, we will be convinced by it'

But the fact that one view is true does not necessarily mean that the other cause is wrong, and that an error in one cause does not necessarily mean that the other cause is correct ..

The pluralistic perspective assumes that for any single event or group of causes, they share in causing it with varying degrees and different effects

Perhaps one person says that the price of the phone is affected by the demand for it, while another says that it is affected by the production cost

And in fact, from the perspective of pluralism, it is affected by these two causes, as well as millions of other causes, rising and falling ..

Therefore, when you are thinking about setting up a plan or starting a project and you are thinking about one of the reasons for failure

Do not stand with a narrow perspective and ignorance of the perspective of diversity

The cause of the problem was not this, but this

Therefore, we should not do this, but do this

We must think deeply about the matter and consider all expected and possible causes to find solutions for them. There may be priorities, but certainly, this does not prevent us from looking comprehensively...

Ignorance of the perspective of diversity can be one of the reasons for the failure of both individuals and institutions. When institutions start a project and do not achieve their goal, they should not look at only one method to increase this goal, such as increasing promotional advertisements, but also to increase the quality of their products or services and to welcome their customers well, and so on...

For example, comprehensive nursing care, spiritually, physically, and morally, is one of the applications of the perspective of diversity that began in 1980, and there are many others...

If a patient's complaint is not necessarily caused by inflammation or something else, but perhaps returning to the primary cause leads us to psychological problems or a lack of nutrition or environmental conditions, then when thinking about the problem, we return to think about all possible problems, whether they have a direct effect on our belief or not, on the apparent problem...

And solving these problems that appear to us in the end leads to reducing the main problem. As for people, you are ignorant of the perspective of pluralism. It may make you look that the point of start needs money and money needs a previous success and the circle revolves, but the perspective of pluralism is that you have many capabilities and start using these capabilities Partially with a gradual increase, it begins to move from the failure circle. I have no money. I will not work. I will not earn money to the circle of success

I have money and I work and I am well evaluated and I get confidence so I get a job and money ...

Conditions

The problem of the criminal conditions may seem one of the problems that lead institutions to fail, and this is true. This term is known in the field of institutions more than individuals, and it means this value that companies pay in case of non -implementation of what was agreed with other companies, and this is one of the reasons for unjustified failure

It does not mean that the company has entered into a contract and committed to a penalty clause that it will fail, but not considering those penalty clauses is the intended reason...

When a construction company decides to obtain an execution contract for a specific facility and enters into a penalty clause for non-execution, 5 times what it would have earned from executing the facility itself... The matter is really strange, it is actually a guarantee for the contracting company's right to execute the project, but not more than paying 120 percent of the amount if the full contract value has been paid, or 20 percent if no payments have been made or what compensates for those amounts...

Some companies see the penalty clause as just numbers on paper and that it will only be paid in the case of execution, so why be afraid, let it be 10 or 15 times what the problem...?

Simply, the problem is that you do not live alone in this life; you live on land within a country that has its rights and laws that change, and perhaps you agreed to this contract based on certain conditions, and suddenly the conditions changed, such as a tax or even the execution prices changed, or the like...

If so, you are not the only one who decides, you will either fulfill what you promised or not, but many external factors are at play, and when you decide to ignore those values considering them as numbers on paper, you are risking much more than what you might gain.

The matter is similar for individuals in the context of the marital property list project.

Some parents may say that it is the daughter's right and a guarantee of her rights, while the husbands see perhaps that as "Why should I be afraid, I won't pay it as long as we are in agreement...?"

Who forgets the partners of the wife in marriage?

Yes ...

For the wife when she is before marriage may show kindness and extravagance that she possesses for her husband, but what after marriage and appear as she is and her mother interferes greedily for her expenses and needs and speaks to her seeking destruction if her father demanded a lot of money from the list and if she saw a divorce from her husband as good, she is the winner ..

But you must not sign anything other than what you own or at least less than that

As for talking about it being just a signature and it will not pay if so why sign and do you have ten times what you paid for the marriage in case of divorce ..?

The conditional failure is one of the reasons for failure that is related to opportunities, as some people look at what they gain from marriage and deals and ignore what they may pay in case of a problematic situation

The essence of opportunities is to invest with what you have, not to borrow and take loans and debts, as this is nothing but an investment for the lenders and not for you

Excess Quality

If one rocket of a certain type of nuclear weapons is capable of destroying life on Earth, why do we need four or five of them?

And if a phone is of a certain reliability and quality, why do we need a bulletproof phone, for example? ..?

Why might we need a shoe that lasts 7 years for a child, while they might need a new one in seven months, not because it is torn but because the child's foot has grown and needs a bigger shoe.. ?

Some people have a mistaken understanding of quality, thinking it is the best in performance, the longest-lasting, and the best in all its features, while ignoring the element of price in quality ..

Modern concept of quality tends to be the best things in performance for the price.

For example, what about two pairs of shoes worth 40 Egyptian pounds each, that last the same age and provide the same comfort as one pair of shoes for 100 pounds...

So the two pairs of shoes are cheaper and of higher quality...

Mania for quality may have affected many and is one of the reasons for failure...

It applies to companies and even to countries...

There is no need to buy these dumb products most of the time, like the product that is food mixed with gold or its protein content is four times that of normal cattle ... or the like

Even in manufacturing, some companies may have an obsession with quality and they try to achieve the highest quality in the traditional sense and proportionally to how many people will need it

And people are not immune to this problem; some also find themselves completing a programming project or the like and are afraid to present it ... why ...?

Because he wants to wait for it to be reviewed until it is the highest quality

It is not necessary for review, but this does not mean that your life should be edited according to a book and published only after your death, or not published at all...

Quality madness or even misunderstanding it is one of the reasons for failure for individuals and companies, whether you are evaluating a product for purchase or producing and selling it...

Think deeply and broadly...

Which is better...?

Display my products now and innovate them in the future and earn or should I continue to innovate throughout my life...?

Do I need this pants that will live for a hundred years while I do not expect anyone to live a hundred years...

It's funny but it's far from your calculations to look at quality in exchange for the price; I need a pants that might be good but not for a hundred years.

Measure that in the field of your education as a person or your contracts as a company.

Chapter nine

This chapter discusses the causes of failure related to challenges, and we mention sixteen, including ignorance of challenges, ignoring challenges, wasting time in complaining, misunderstanding of challenges, temporary solutions to challenges, black outlook, irregular assessments, accurate reports, import solutions, personality, challenges, and fire extinguishing perspective with fire, and everyone's perspective. All and the circle of revenge, the perspective of absolute suspicion, the perspective of all of the whole, and the perspective of the ship

Ignorance of challenges

Ignorance of challenges is that you do not know the challenges facing you in the present or the future, and whether this ignorance was intentionally, that is, you did not make a plan to reveal the challenges and get to know them or that you do not understand the subject of challenges from the basis and this is for individuals and institutions alike.

It is one of the reasons for failure because it prevents you from setting up a plan to overcome those challenges because undoubtedly, any plan you set up without knowing those challenges from the beginning .. ?!

In management science, starting any project requires conducting an analysis called "SWOT," which includes among its four parts identifying challenges and opportunities

This is because understanding challenges is not a��� part, but it starts since the idea is born ..

Two or three days ago, I presented an idea to a friend ..

Perhaps I promised him a discussion, but .. He did not know how many problems and challenges in front of him were, so his plan was simple, that is not enough to create a plan

Knowing the challenges, you may need consultations, opinions and experiences, and not just just to hold the paper and write the challenges that can meet you ..

After this information, this begins to determine and extract more simple challenges than the first challenges, and this is in order to develop the plan to overcome it.

And even man

Every period, possibly every six months at most, one needs to sit with himself and identify the challenges he faces, such as lack of money or family problems or housing problems or even work problems or global problems that affect him...

Therefore, ignorance of the challenges is the first step to what follows, which is neglecting the challenges and thus not making a plan for solving them, and consequently failing in what one does as a human...

What is the solution then...?

Understanding and believing that challenges exist and are a part of nature, and that it is necessary to make plans to overcome them, and that these plans do not necessarily eliminate all challenges but to reduce their impact, and that combining and diversifying these plans helps to minimize the impact of those challenges to the greatest extent...

And the challenges are naturally variable and increasing, so that when you think about something, the challenges may simply be a lack of awareness of the idea, a lack of financing, your second job, or even the need for external resources.

But over time, for example, with the outbreak of a pandemic like COVID-19, even marketing has become difficult, and opening a store or place has become difficult to direct people to buy medicine instead of the entertainment you offer, perhaps...

Ignoring challenges

Ignoring challenges is a stage where you are aware of the challenges you face but do not take steps to solve them, either because you do not appreciate those challenges or because you lack the resources...

And in fact, I cannot distinguish between ignorance of the challenges and ignoring them, for in both cases, you have not taken the step to solve it and will not take it.

Whether you know it as in neglect or not as in ignorance

There is no increase...

You do not think about solutions to those challenges...

But why does ignoring challenges lead to failure ...?

Simply, those challenges may be financial and by ignoring them, the company may fail or the individual may go into debt and end up in prison. Perhaps the person who does not understand that the problem is not having enough income is a challenge or who understands it but has not taken any steps to solve it is on the path to a profound failure...

And the other who has a challenge in eating a circle of customers or friends, whether he understands this or not, is also on the path to failure because over time, the problem will worsen. Instead of losing one or two customers daily, the number and rate will increase even more.

And even on a personal level, a lack of friends is not just a trivial reason for problems but a reason to enter seclusion and depression and a decrease in abilities. Just as in the previous example, the person in times of trouble will turn to a friend for help or to lend him, but with the loss of these friends, his capabilities and relationships decrease.

Wasting time complaining

Every challenge requires a lot of time to know that it exists, then another time to understand the problem, and even more time to solve this challenge and overcome it

And when you continue to complain, you have wasted time knowing the challenge and understanding it, and instead of spending the most important time solving the challenge, you spend time in complaints that do not solve anything

The matter may be understood on a narrow scale that when the problem is something specific to me, I should not complain, and complaining is possible if the problem or challenge is, for example, in the rudeness of colleagues or administrative problems with you at work or the like...

But one of the general reasons for failure for people is wasting time in complaining even if you do not have solutions for the problem because that complaint that you have no solution for is not a challenge but an environmental problem, and the solution is often to get out of that environment...

And you do not need to repeat the complaint repeatedly to the managers with you to tell them that a colleague comes late to work and you have to wait longer than your time, or that one of those who work with you harms the reputation of the institution, which harms you as a part of the institution...

It is natural for the responsible persons in that institution to be aware of these problems and monitor them to see if they are indeed a problem, or if they are a one-time exception with a valid excuse, you are not required to complain either, because by doing so, you are creating a problem out of a non-problem...

If the problem is temporary stress or a one-time delay by a passing colleague or a non-recurring mistake, then there is no need for a complaint because it does not happen often...

And if it happens repeatedly, there is no complaint because the occurrence of this without the awareness of the person responsible for the place in itself is an environmental problem ..

The complaint itself creates problems

And if there are repeated mistakes against you, when you complain, "you add fuel to the fire," perhaps you have become the disliked person in that place because of that complaint

And perhaps you have repeated this reason many times ..

Beware ..

You do not have the others to change them, but you have yourself to change and bring to an appropriate place. And if all places do not suit you, create an appropriate place.

Do not continue to complain about the years and curse the days for the few opportunities, for perhaps you now understand the meaning of opportunities ..

Persisting in complaining, if it is not one of the reasons for failure, is just a waste of time, but it also wastes relationships. Whether you complain about someone or to someone, both will hate dealing with you. If you complain to a friend, they will get tired, and if you complain to someone else, they will get angry and plot against you ..

And even in the most beautiful ways of complaining, by the general complaint that I call or as it is said by the advisor, "This is beautiful, but it lacks just this, but it is beautiful "

Some may see it as a good thing, but even so, it may provoke envy in people in the long run... But it is much better than the traditional complaint.

Therefore, wasting time in complaining is one of the reasons for the failure of people in all cases.

As for institutions, they cannot complain because merely announcing that the company is going bankrupt or that it has problems will not increase profits or even maintain them, and will not stir the emotions of anyone. Perhaps some people complain in the hope that someone will show compassion and solve the problem.

But the announcement of errors by companies may be acceptable, but the approach of announcing internal problems means the end of the company itself, as well as the institutions...

Misunderstanding of the challenges

Misunderstanding of the challenges may be confused with a lack of knowledge of the challenges, but perhaps this is not a big problem because confusing them in themselves is not a problem; but the problem is not understanding the reasons for that...

Misunderstanding of the challenges is not just a lack of knowledge of the challenges or ignoring that you know them, but a confusion of challenges due to ignoring the concept of challenges from the outset, which makes an opportunity, for example, seem like a challenge to you, and this may absorb your time to overcome it as a challenge through the preparation of a plan and analysis of those challenges, and so on, which are essentially not challenges...

Challenges are those problems that you encounter while striving to achieve something in the path towards accomplishing your goals ..

And as a result, the definition can be phrased as the obstacles that need to be prepared for on the path to success ..

For example, if you decided to start a public bath company in Egypt ..

Perhaps you will find that the challenges are the lack of a payment culture for entering the bath in the street ..

The second is perhaps sufficient spaces to implement the project in the squares

The third is the method of payment for the service without any excuse "No jokes or living money, there is no excuse .."

The fourth is the elderly and those who have no shelter, who pays for them ..?

But on the other hand, other things will not be challenges despite the fact that they seem to be so

Like who cleans those places because the metro, for example, has experience in operating these places and they are cleaned easily

And transporting organic waste, many other companies work in the field easily...

So, misunderstanding the challenges as the steps makes you plan for every step, which is unacceptable...

But clear and correct understanding of the challenges as just the issues makes you focus on the real issues and obstacles instead of wasting time on matters that happen simply like hiring a cleaner for the place or contracting an organic waste transportation company to dispose of it...

Temporary solutions for challenges

When we know about the challenges, perhaps the easiest choice is a quick solution to hide the matter, or even to satisfy the immediate need of the matter...

I completely agree that in the case of an injured person in a traffic accident, we do not need to ask about the cause of the accident and trace the cause... And I agree that in the case of a person in a coma due to a lack of oxygen to the brain as a result of anemia, it is not the first solution to trace the causes and look at each cause behind the cause...

But it is logical to implement quick solutions in these times

But these solutions are not originally solutions, but rather a stop-gap for the problem until solutions are put in place...

By giving you glucose solution or even a blood transfusion or fitting an oxygen device for the person or rescuing the injured, you have not solved the fundamental problem...

Because it is not reasonable for the injured person to return home and for accidents to recur despite this happening and it is not reasonable for the anemia patient to return home until he has another attack and comes for an oxygen session...

But the solution is to request tests to find out the causes of that anemia and its treatment... and the causes of the accident...

If narrow on the road, it is expanded; if young, patrols are deployed; if there is a lack of leadership abilities, the problem is resolved ... perhaps it is a mix of all this, and the integration of solutions here is required.

Therefore, any problem that requires a radical solution, some problems and challenges may require a solution before being radical ... to achieve the radical solution.

Therefore, temporary solutions are those that reduce the harm but do not prevent it or interrupt it.

Therefore, temporary solutions are not the cause of failure but reliance on them alone.

It is strange that temporary solutions, although they are a cause of failure when relied upon, may still be required before the fundamental solutions in emergency situations.

No matter whether it is an individual who has a sudden problem without prior warning or even an institution

It is necessary first, as it was said to us

"Save lives first.. "

The person who stops you at the half of the night asks you for money with a coercion is threatened with a weapon or the company that loses one of the main supply chains contracts and has requests and reservations

They both need a quick solution that does not think at first about the cause of the problem

But once the urgent and urgent problem is solved, the time comes to a deep analysis to understand what happened

Sometimes in companies and institutions the matter is different

Perhaps specialized teams are preferable in emergency work

and others specialize in strategic planning to avoid such problems .. and challenges

The "Black View"

The "Black View" as one of the causes of failure is to surrender to problems and challenges as if there are no solutions to them ..

This student who planned to study medicine in one of the universities and failed, and this girl who agreed to a groom for herself but he left her, and that mother who planned not to buy furniture for the house but the rise in prices prevented her...

Life is full of challenges, and perhaps the challenges we face are similar to those faced by others, so we consider them ordinary or even more severe pain and harshness, so we consider life to be dark and cruel...

One of the reasons for failure is feeling the darkness of the situation...

I am with you, we are not in the best place, and no one living on the planet is an angel...

One of the reasons for the pessimistic view is the illusion ..

The illusion that makes us think others are better than us, they imagine themselves through camera filters, adorned with artificial colors on their faces ..

This girl who was left by her fiancé when she was in the third year of college might not have been killed by loneliness; she lives with her parents, but her nerves were killed, and her pain was turned into that pessimistic view, that word that a classmate said to her, "My fiancé is not depriving me of anything," or "My husband does this .."

Some young people complain playfully and mockingly about their situation on professional social networks like LinkedIn and say, "I feel like a mosquito every time I go there .."

Not because of his lack of skills, but because his skills, when compared to the offered ones, seem minimal... Perhaps his skills are the best...

The pessimistic outlook is not always due to a lack of effort or limited resources, nor is it due to increased problems, but rather because of placing yourself in comparisons with people who may sometimes be fictional, just images with filters or followers for money, or even early and unhappy marriage...

The pessimistic or negative outlook is one of the causes of failure related to challenges because it exaggerates the challenges you face without taking steps to solve them...

And it is not because of the magnitude and size of the challenges, but rather because your challenges, compared to others, seem great...

Perhaps others do not show problems as they seem to you, and this is not that they have no challenges but perhaps because they spend time solving challenges or at least they do not waste time complaining ..

Whether you are a person, a company, or an institution, a negative outlook can end your life .. Companies when they transition from companies that set plans to companies that monitor the fall of others

And when company leaders turn to a lack of hope, this despair is passed on to the employees ..

And the same applies to individuals ..

Therefore, stop these comparisons to free yourself from the negative outlook and instead of comparing yourself to the best, remember how many times a person has put you through this and came out recovered

Irregular evaluations

The treatment is a poison!

If used at the wrong time, although it may be a lifesaver in other times ..

We are in life as individuals and institutions, and we need to use materials and actions, and perhaps procedures based on certain evaluations. ... If you come to a patient and notice that their blood sugar is lower than normal, they may be injected with glucose or something else. But if they call for glucose and remain connected to it, they will die.

It is not a lack of glucose, but an excess.

We are on Earth, and perhaps on other planets, we do not have an action that works for everything or a material that works for every situation, but rather its absence from what is undesirable, and I have said about what is undesirable... And these boundaries differ.

This may be superficial information, but why is there an inconsistency in evaluations, one of the reasons for failure?

Simply because irregular evaluations prevent you from knowing the current situation, whether it is for the patient, the market, or your capabilities

Whether you are learning a new language or creating a product to sell

Your evaluation of customer opinions and touchpoints will change what you need...

Your evaluation of a good employee's performance ensures that they continue to be good... Many employees in companies, for example, start with the best performance and then what...

After a few months, they gradually become lazy, indifferent, and procrastinate. And when you set their salary and tasks, you initially set them based on their competence, and without your continuous evaluation, they will retain their positions without performing.

Perhaps in some countries, there is an idea called "demotion..." or -I don't find a translation for it in my Arabic language-.. which means descending in rank to the position before it. But this is not present in many of our cultures. For example, some people, as Muhammad Sabahy said, "If they don't work, they won't make mistakes and will be promoted."

Why are evaluations not based on a systematic approach, but rather on drawing attention?

This person who doesn't work but gets promoted is evidence that some people do not have a clear evaluation schedule, or even an unclear one, but what is important is the schedule and consistency.

And some depend on the circumstances; he evaluates the employee's state of crisis only and ends their service, but if their performance deteriorates and diminishes, he does not pay attention to this in the evaluation or consider their performance, and therefore the promotion remains because there is no evaluation; he has not made a mistake because he has not worked...

Consistency in evaluations is not because you only evaluate when writing, but because you might forget the evaluation process...

Humans have memory, but also have the skill in writing to schedule those evaluations...

Whether it's for companies, as we said, with employees or for markets, requesting it or the quality standards practiced...

It is strange that humans do not exist only to ensure the continuation of performance as it was

Because in our era, progress is present and it is not enough just to maintain your level, but also to remain in need of development, and development is faster than others. I am not saying a pessimistic view, but a pursuit of improvement as long as you take steps instead of despair and complaining...

Reliability of inaccurate reports

Of course, solving problems and facing challenges by setting up plans requires collecting information and analyzing it, etc. But what if that information is inaccurate or biased...?

And what about that data collection method ... ?!

What if the university wanted to collect the students' opinions on a course or the performance of a doctoral student and distributed papers to collect data before an important exam ...?

Or what if the person responsible for collecting the data is the one being evaluated himself ...?

And what if the person collecting the data still relies on manual calculations and forgets to add numbers or something else ...?

Then what if it is adopted that this information is real and it expresses the problem and plans are made based on it ... ?

Here, the reliability of inaccurate reports is one of the causes of failure because they lead you to waste on unnecessary things or perhaps neglect aspects or give a wrong view of performance

And with a little bit of the love of appearing great, some who collect data and neglect or lack of interest and motivation to those who provide the data ...

And with limited time and the lack of using simple methods for collecting data

With a little error in setting up the current assessment questions due to incorrect reliance on previous assessments

And the circle continues

Incorrect information leads to wrong decisions and gathers more incorrect data ..

But in institutions, the subject may be more complex ..

Perhaps the cause of the problem is someone who pretends to try to solve it or even tries it without realizing that he is the cause of the problem.

Perhaps some do not have a proper understanding of the foundations of administrative science, while others understand that administration is just a practice and that a computer science degree is enough to manage a computer college or a computer import company, ignoring a related and integrated science called administrative science and another called statistics.

Some fail to collect data for the company and improve it, and then decide to put in place a solution and train everyone who works with him... Who trains them...?!

It's himself ...!

Let's return to the point that was previously mentioned

one of the reasons for failure is the reliance on people and institutions on inaccurate information, and therefore they set plans that fail or need to be revised every day, so the main ideas coincide and time is wasted

Importing solutions

one of the most famous problem-solving methods is to consider how others solve problems, but some understand that this consideration is merely the transfer of the experience and transfer of ideas with the forms and the entire solution as if it were a "sacred description and a successful model without modification or detail or review .. "

This is not a rejection of the success of solutions, but rather a difference in circumstances...

For example, the Western educational system will never be suitable for Arab countries, and perhaps designing a train in a northern European country will not succeed in equatorial countries due to the difference in temperature...

And even the communication system in some companies may not succeed in others due to cultural differences... And perhaps due to differences in spatial and temporal circumstances...

Simply, people who are making profits buy things of lesser value, and there are expectations that this will increase...

While the foolish wait for the rich to make profits in a particular thing before starting to buy it

Some, when Bitcoin appeared as a cryptocurrency, looked at the expectations and analyses and dared to buy a large amount

And what next ..

When the price went up, they started selling it ..

Here were the fools

They waited until the success of the rise in the price of betaine ..

Then they decided to import the experience and buy betaine at high prices

Then what .. ?

Its price has collapsed somewhat from its peak.

So the real profit is in the difference and creating new ideas, even if it is just a simple different feature.

You might find that Twitter and WeChat do what Facebook does as a social networking platform, but the differences between them have made both of them succeed.

One of the people I was talking to was about designing a website to showcase an institution he supports...

Suddenly, he wished for a dream and started asking me ..

"Can you create a platform like Telegram ..?!"

The question was strange .. not just because I didn't know and hadn't thought of doing this

but also because I was amazed that he was trying to replicate something as a product for himself .. He is simply trying to reinvent the wheel without modification just because he saw that the Telegram platform is successful ..

Some people think that following the same paths of success leads to success, but I tell you, usually not...

Why...?

Because whoever walked the path of success before you took what was in it and moved ahead of you by his lead; he may have possessed loyalty from his customers and experience, while you compete with nothing but imitation...

Another reason why importing solutions can be a reason for failure is that you might import one solution and find, for example, that in this solution they use a specific material, and you import the solution and decide to transfer the solution with all its elements and decide to use the same material...

you will find that the use of that material was due to its availability there when the solution emerged

perhaps you are here deciding to replace it with another one that is available to you .. but this is just because I am discussing this with you, but usually, what happens is that the person decides to transfer the experience as it is, including if a specific material is used, decide to use it, and if it is not available, import it the solutions when put in place are based on what is available and not that we should provide what we need for the solution, but rather build the solution on what is available

personalizing the challenges

Personalizing challenges is a very broad concept as one of the causes of failure ... It includes seeing obstacles as deliberate and facing them alone, and includes considering the problem as resulting from a specific person's situation and that it resulted from everyone. It also includes the sentence "This is not my specialty, I am responsible for such and such in the company and that's it..."

Whether you are an individual or an institution, personalizing challenges is one of the causes of failure you will face...

As for companies...

If all employees do not understand the institution's goals and believe in and agree with them, then every problem that occurs, every loss they face, every dissatisfied customer, and every fall of the institution will begin with every employee talking about their role and what they did, or not, and blaming others, or not, and being content with the sentence "I am specialized in this, I have no claim..."

The matter may also be a personification of situations between individuals, for example, Ahmed and Nermine work at the same company and due to an error on Ahmed's part in assessing or dealing with Nermine, the situation turns into a conflict

Personal conflict

In which Nermine rejects any proposal not because of its badness but because it is for Ahmed, and it turns into a tool that harms the company just for harming Ahmed, and here the personification of challenges is one of the causes of failure

But at the level of individuals

When I heard that sentence, I didn't know how a real sentence could be ..

Someone told me

"If no one greets you, it is not necessarily because of you, but perhaps for thousands of other reasons .."

When you look at a person saying a sentence or talking about you or the like, you don't realize that he has a life bigger than yours and deals with thousands of others

\nAs soon as you think he is targeting you in something, the topic turns into a squabble..\n

\nAnd personalizing challenges on a personal level, for example, when a man offers a good deal on a product, but just because of your rivalry with him, you say, "No... I'll buy it from someone else for more money..." is foolishness and personalization..\n

\nMaybe this helps in strategies..\n

\nBut if the product is the product itself and the rivalry is just your own trivial rivalry, then it is one of the causes of failure.\n

When you decide to exclude a successful man from your management out of fear that he might surpass you, that is backwardness. For when you are in a good position, an employee is better than being a manager of a failing institution.

Your efforts to maintain your position by getting rid of the competent or even excluding the company of the truth because you only like to be the best friend is a personality of challenges and a cause for failure.

Viewing the fire extinguishing the fire with fire

It may seem ridiculous to see this team building a wall around the city while they are building a wall, and after they finish it, they start the second one and begin to take components of the wall to build the second one...?!

But some people still do this

Some people, if they decide to overcome a challenge, create another even greater challenge

This person who borrows an amount from the bank and has a loan that is difficult for them to pay and takes another to pay off the first one, is just putting out a fire with fire

And this person who finds himself lost and confused in his problems and turns to drinking alcohol to forget what troubles him at night is also putting out a fire with fire...

This young man who felt the narrowness of the world around him and decided to end his life by suicide is actually extinguishing fire with fire.

And that girl who delayed her marriage and decided to partially strip off some of her clothes to be bright and attractive is actually extinguishing fire with fire.

This young man or girl who was abandoned by a friend after giving something up decided to return the betrayal, which is actually extinguishing fire with fire.

Many situations actually express this perspective in full, which is facing the challenge with a challenge different from others.

The matter is if it creates another challenge even if it solves a partial challenge of the first one

And even companies sometimes fall into the same mistake by deciding to make a product similar to another product and find the product losing and reduce its price and increase its production and reduce the demand due to the abundance of supply and some companies remain stubborn and revengeful as after this ..

But just thinking about solving another problem or giving up another one

Decide to increase the quality of the product and raise its price twice or decide to decrease the price and reduce the quality by a quarter and half

If the matter requires a graduated solution, you solve the problem and try to prevent other problems with more thoughtful plans, rather than reconciling with a colleague and losing the other or sacrificing quality or price for the other or destroying a wall to build another...

So simply put, the perspective of extinguishing fire with fire is giving up some good for less good or accepting some problems in exchange for avoiding others... This idea is one of the reasons for failure because it simply replaces the real solution with a false one, and thereby becomes one of the reasons for failure for individuals or institutions...

The perspective of all against all

The perspective of cooperation is often difficult to implement, especially with differing views and sometimes the absence of any vision at all. For cooperation to exist, there must be agreed-upon principles to establish a framework for problem occurrence, and this is because the problem will inevitably exist, which is a natural thing...

But today, with these differences and ambiguity in dealing, you will find the most comprehensive perspective globally through international and institutional relations, or even through individuals, that it is "everyone against everyone," and perhaps this is the title of one of the books.

But the idea simply is that you sit with five working against others, then with a part of others working against the rest...

Some consider it an extraordinary skill because you are capable of deception and working with everyone against everyone, but this wise person who sees you deny the beauty of others and abandon them easily will be completely convinced that you are not dependent on or trusted by you...

Also, because here you are not only untrusted but also trying to prove that you really work with this person against that person and work with another against the first.. And when the truth is revealed, everyone will be against you.. And this is what the Egyptian film depicted...

So why is the perspective of everyone against everyone is one of the reasons for people's failure

As for the individuals, you are agreed with each one with the opinion and works as if you are a colleague for him, as this loses your clear orientations sometimes and may make you get lost with them and also engage with them in actions against some, the second matter is that even the people who work with them know that you have no safety and the third thing is to consume times at work on several sides .. It is better, if you start thinking, which one is with him and any of them against and one of the most close with my thought that you do not help with him ...

As for companies, within each company, employees who work for temporary periods and work against a specific company with employees who can leave the work that can expose you to accountability simply, especially if there are joint agreements

Here, the question is easier because people have returned their communication is unofficial. Perhaps what is more sound or video is made. As for companies, there are formal e -mails, memoranda of understanding, hostility, and issues that cost companies a lot, so perhaps the gain of the years is paying as a fine, punishment, or even compensation

Always remember that the secret is that if someone knows it, there is a possibility of it being leaked, and the more people who know the secret, the greater the likelihood of it being leaked.

Those communications in the perspective of everyone against everyone are one of the reasons for the collapse of relationships between companies or even customer trust.

Cycle of revenge

One of the causes of failure is allowing others to direct you simply because they made a mistake against you...

I was just talking a little while ago with someone who is like many who say "We will treat you well after that" Many of us say it...

One time, I was asked this question...

Doctor and academic who stole a scientific research from a student and published it under his name...

The poor girl kept asking what should I do...?

Some talk about revenge, while others may speak of tolerance...

And some remained silent, as if the situation.....!

Indeed, revenge may be the first option presented to the majority...

But what comes after revenge and how should revenge be carried out.....?

Stealing research is the act of stealing research for something new, it may seem fair, but in reality, it is a folly and a cause of failure ... Do you know why ... ?

Because you abandon your principles for mere revenge ...

You will steal research from a doctor or start to insult him or her or just for revenge ...

Revenge is a foolish way; this person stole what you did and toiled over, and you allow him also to take revenge on your thoughts ...

Here is the optimal solution

It is better to grieve, be calm, and think than to act impulsively and give an arbitrary response

Here, you need not to blame anyone but to blame yourself a little and then to move forward with a new search, instead of sitting in sadness over this search and thinking about its response...

Think of creating something else, moving forward, and avoiding falling into the same mistake...

Simply because revenge makes you deviate from your path...

You might be traveling to a distant country...

There are probably solutions in front of you...

The first one is to get off your journey and start replying to the insult...

And the second is to complete your path to your goal .. and your destination ..

The first is when you descend and return, you have wasted time from your time and delayed your journey, and the second is that you ignored and skipped over it, not for it, but for focusing on what you want ..

The idea of tolerance may seem futile to some and foolish to some ..

But tolerance for us is not for this sinner, but for you ..

Imagine how much time you spend thinking about who you hate and thinking about replying to them and thinking about what they did ...?!

It is if you are occupied with achieving what you want and it gets you into a cycle of revenge "If you hurt him, he will hurt you, and you will become a hurtful enemy .. "

In the past, the cycle of revenge might have been more intense ... but it sometimes starts with a simple situation and develops in a spiral manner ..

Someone didn't greet you... they didn't see you.

You decided not to invite them to your daughter's wedding because they didn't greet you. They didn't attend your daughter's wedding and responded by not attending your father's funeral. The cycle continues until it leads to the destruction of property from hatred on both sides.

As for individuals, the situation is clear, and as for institutions, companies also, when they enter competition, often spiral into revenge. Some lower the prices of their products to lose a bid to another, while others lower prices out of revenge. Some buy all the stock from a dealer, despite not being able to market it, just to prevent the other from profiting, and the cycle of revenge continues.

This causes people to lose their values, goals, and vision in the pursuit of revenge and winning a fictional race.

Thus, the cycle of revenge becomes a

clearer cause of failure for both individuals and institutions, although its initial impact is on individuals.

Perspective of Absolute Doubt

I talked a lot about doubt in my book Principles of Control in Contemporary Thought.

But to summarize the concept of absolute doubt, it's doubt in everything. This is a strange matter—if you don't have facts or constants to believe in, how do you build your ideas or draw new conclusions from what you doubt?

Thus, the concept of absolute doubt is one of the reasons for failure because you can't trust anything, not even yourself.

Here, you start to doubt your decisions and choices, and you find yourself revisiting what you do.

However, this isn't just about doubt; it's a kind of doubt based on certain points of certainty. Your faith—whether in religion or non-religion—is based on ideas firmly embedded in your mind about yourself, others, what you do, and what you need to do.

Absolute doubt, on the other hand, is like a moving cloud that is not anchored to anything; it just drifts—though even clouds are held together by gravity and water molecule cohesion.

Therefore, every person or institution must have a clear vision of their formation, goals, principles, and axioms in place. They should refer back to these axioms when in doubt. For instance, when you doubt someone's performance, you return to the company's goal: does this person meet the goals or not? Similarly, in your personal goals, you need to build trust in your religion, your belief in it, then trust in yourself, and then trust others based on these ideas.

This is because both people and institutions are not isolated from the world; they need trust to build relationships and ease interactions.

Perspective of Part of the Whole

Sometimes, we stand and think, analyzing which cause is the problem, and try to pick just one of the causes, differentiating them by fractions. It's as if the cause of the problem must be just one thing, and the problem should come from only one source, and so we focus on solving the problem.

When two colleagues fight at work, an investigation begins to find who is at fault and to determine the cause. But we forget that the cause might be from both sides—perhaps the first was more at fault, but by a fraction, yet the second could have tolerated and resolved the issue without the fight.

We forget that every problem has many causes, and solving the problem, even with punishment for the wrongdoer, sometimes requires rehabilitating the one who made the lesser mistake.

Simply put, we forget that in the workplace, if Ahmed arrives at 8 AM and leaves at 8 PM, and Ibrahim works in his shift, this is illogical. Both need time to hand over work, and thus Ahmed must start earlier than 8 AM and Ibrahim should stay a few minutes later than 8 PM.

We forget that in any matter where boundaries are just a fictional line with no true value, the problem arises.

Simply, we need flexibility. Ahmed's role might be to work at a level lower than his full capacity so he can use his full potential when a problem arises.

Some managers focus on the maximum that an employee can do and order them to do it, forgetting to create that zone of flexibility.

What about in emergencies?

Can this person, who usually works at full capacity, increase their effort in an emergency?

You may have everything scheduled and claim there's enough time, but what about disasters?

Do you have non-essential tasks that you can delay for more important emergent tasks?

In management science, there's always a concept called "buffer time" or "balance time," which compensates for any shortage or surplus of time in work.

So why does focusing on part of the whole lead to failure?

Simply because you look at the profit that comes from setting fixed working hours (12 hours for each person), ignoring the reality.

You look at forcing all employees to work at full capacity, forgetting what to do in emergencies.

Thus, resources and time need to be allocated for emergencies, problems, and delays in delivery.

Perhaps you look at part of the picture and see that work has been running smoothly for years, thinking nothing will change. But you don't know what the future holds.

You need to look at the bigger picture, and since you can't see it all, always make room for flexibility.

You may need a day to complete a task—give yourself a day and a half.

You need 50 workers—hire 55.

Even if a company typically expects to store one ton of resources, make sure the warehouse can hold one and a half tons at the least. Always consider the bigger picture.

Perspective of the Hole in the Boat

Here, we talk about the idea of some people creating challenges in society.

Some see creating a hole in the boat as a simple way to get water, especially if the boat is in a fresh river.

Others view them as free as long as they puncture their own part of the boat, even helping them, just to keep them from asking others for water.

A third category stays silent as if they don't even consider it a problem.

It may seem foolish, like a story from fiction.

But it's a mindset rooted in some people's attempts to overcome challenges.

Challenges are inevitable, and only successful people overcome them. But they do so correctly, not by creating new challenges to overcome the first one.

The idea of the hole in the boat reflects one of the foolish and imaginary solutions to overcoming challenges.

Why?

Because, simply, they're thinking of the problem as the lack of water. Instead of choosing one of the correct ways to gather water from the river into the boat, they decide to make a hole in the boat.

Not only that, but some help them, as if keeping them from asking for water themselves helps. It's like a man helping his neighbor rob a third neighbor so that this neighbor won't ask for water.

It's not just foolishness; even silence is not an indication that you're immune to the problem. You didn't puncture the boat or help puncture it, but you stayed silent while the boat sank.

Thus, the solution is either to stop the hole from being made or abandon the boat.

But often, the best solution is to prevent the hole from being made, either by advising or by force.

Sometimes, it's about providing an alternative way to collect water from the river or even doing it yourself.

Trust me, sometimes carrying the burden is not because you like the burden, but because the donkey doesn't understand the danger ahead.

But remember the principle: prevent the donkey from entering your house in the first place.

Whether it's a project, a ship, or an institution, choosing the right partners is better than enduring them or abandoning them.

You may live your life tolerating your spouse for the sake of the children, but the better solution is to be cautious in your choice, or maybe even to separate.

So the perspective of the hole in the boat is a misguided way to solve a problem, and in order to survive, you should not stay silent. Either abandon or stop it, even if it's at your expense. You are prioritizing, maybe even compromising—not because you're wrong, but because you know that foolish people don't understand the danger.

Don't say, "We're all in this together," but instead consider that to avoid failure, you might have to prevent the failure of those around you as well.

Chapter 10

This chapter discusses the causes of failure related to value and its measurements and considerations, and mentions ten reasons for it, including ignorance of value, market valuation, ignoring the missing value, ignoring the validity of value, poor storage of value, high inflation rates, the benchmark value, the wrong appreciation of value, algebraic calculation of value, and uncalculated values.

Ignorance of Value

In any task we undertake, plan for, evaluate, or establish principles for, and in every sentence we discuss with another person, we must view things with this value. Even when it comes to human beings, their value is more complex than material possessions. However, ignorance of value is one of the reasons for failure, as it makes us incapable of properly evaluating the things around us.

How much should we pay for this product, and how much should we sell it for? How much time should we spend developing ourselves? And how worthwhile will this be?

Value is the measure we use to assess something based on our need for it at a specific time. Ignorance of value could mean not knowing the capabilities of what we own or even what we can do. Many people think that starting a project simply requires money, and because they don't have money, they think they are failures. They may need a loan, but since they don't have a project, they can't get the loan, and here a vicious cycle of failure begins. Simply because they ignore value.

They don't know their capabilities. They may not have money, and that may be true or false, but what is certain is that they have things that hold value. Think about your relationships, your ability to read, or your ability to sing, or even your ability to work well with children. Think if you're skilled at cooking. Think about the value in your old books and reflect for a while. You'll find many things of value that you didn't recognize.

Maybe you don't see the value in your phone, from which you read the book, or even if it's printed. Consider the potential of your body and what you're capable of doing. Do you know that just by speaking, you have value? You can rely on that to provide voice-over services. What if you're a university student or have a LinkedIn account? These are values you might be unaware of, but you can build success upon them.

Think about all the things you have and how you can use them as part of a plan to achieve your goal — that's success. When you say "I don't have money," you're right, but what you have is what matters. It doesn't matter what you don't have. If you focus on what you lack, you'll work on obtaining it, but your main goal will shift to acquiring what you don't have, and you'll enter a circle of envy, hatred, and sadness about what you lack.

Think about how we have two small stones, and we want to make a fire. How do we do it? You may have a LinkedIn account and need a job. You may know how to cook and need a job. Here, the idea begins to emerge through setting goals and determining capabilities. This is the easiest way to start, a method often ignored by those who fail.

But value and understanding it go deeper than this. We're talking about value also as something for sale and exchange. Maybe you're working and offering a service or selling goods. How do you assess the value of what you have, or what you need to pay for?

Market Evaluation:

As one of the reasons for failure, market evaluation traps many people in the bubble of perceived value. Simply put, you look at something through a lens whose magnification you may not know. When you see an advertisement about the benefits or quality of a product being promoted by a celebrity, that person may not have actually seen or tried the product; they are merely promoting it.

Many fall into this trap by believing advertisements, and sometimes it's not even traditional ads that we're used to; many advertisers have begun to refine their methods by persuading. Some focus not on showing benefits but on showing that it is normal for the wealthy to own these products, and you, too, may think that since the rich use it, you should too in order to be rich like them, or at least appear this way.

Market value, simply put, is the value of a product as presented by society. Perhaps a yogurt cup, which doesn't really provide much nourishment, becomes perceived as a complete meal due to advertising. When you convince yourself that this yogurt cup is a full meal, its true value might only be 10 or 15 cents, but you evaluate it based on its market value.

Look at stock market shares; they rise and fall based on people's opinions. Sometimes market evaluation is an issue because some treat the product like currency. What does this mean? It means that you say, "I buy the product as it's priced by the market because when I sell it, I'll sell it at market value, and I won't lose by following market pricing."

Simply put, you're not buying a product; you're buying a commodity. The difference between a commodity and a product is that the product is sold for its ultimate consumption, and although it may change hands between traders, its value is clearer. Commodities, however, vary in value, unlike currency. For example, gold is of fixed value, but paper currency's value is based on supply, demand, and trust.

This means that paper currency is not the same as a product. A product may spoil or lose its value when its use is no longer possible, or it may increase in value because no one else is making it or growing it.

Additionally, sometimes products are market-priced lower than their true value as perceived by our needs. Water and salt, for example, may cost much less than their value to us, simply because they're abundant, while in other places, they are desperately needed.

So, how can we avoid failure stemming from market evaluation? Simply by looking at value based on our need for it and how much is sufficient when you decide to exchange it, without focusing on what others have evaluated it as.

The gold ring on your finger, as a ring, is not worth more than the value of a painted iron ring as an ornament. But its real value, as a currency, comes when you want to sell it. Similarly, a luxurious car is worth much less than what it's sold for when compared to a modest car. Look at the difference in value, as both fulfill the same purpose of getting you to your destination.

In a logical and philosophical dilemma:

Many companies offering website hosting services on cloud storage are actually selling more space than they have! Do you know why? Because many don't understand value in relation to them. Many buy more storage than they need simply because they perceive it as an added value, maybe even for security at times, but not always.

In this case, they've bought something they don't use, and the seller has sold the same thing to others. It's like buying a wallet for one dollar to hold 20 cents. You perceive the wallet's value based on what others think, but you forget that its value for you is just in holding those 20 cents.

Buy only what you need and get only what you need, based on your value for it or its availability — whichever is less.

Ignoring lost cost

In our daily life situations, we often need to determine the value of what we need or do, or even the value of opportunities and challenges. For instance, the value of a television you're buying or the value of a course you're getting for free through a company's grant. The offers may seem tempting, and sometimes you realize the price you're paying, but the hidden part is the sacrifices involved.

We all have the same 24 hours in a day. This free course might seem like a fantastic opportunity, but on the other hand, it will require five days of travel, each day with 8 to 10 hours of attendance, and you might also need to read up on the course material after returning. This is the lost value, for example.

Ignoring this lost value when you gain something could be one of the deep reasons for failure. Many people, when evaluating something, only consider its benefits. This TV you're buying will allow you to watch movies and entertain yourself, but what about the time lost, the electricity, and the space it takes up on the wall?

Your friend may be a loyal companion, but what about the cost of your obligations towards them? Many companies care about memorandums of understanding, which is often a good thing, especially when you understand your commitments to the other party.

The lost value is the amount you pay for something, but not just the money—it's also the time, effort, commitments, and constraints tied to it. The factory you build in a residential area might be a good opportunity for attracting cheap labor without the need for transportation, but what about future development? You've acquired the benefit of a nearby location, but it also limits your future expansion.

Looking at the lost value, I don't consider it a dilemma, but simply recognizing it gives you the chance to understand what you really need. It makes your thinking more logical. Instead of only focusing on the benefits of something, also consider its risks.

This woman may adorn herself with gold, which gives her aesthetic value, but the lost value is the time she spends worrying about being robbed, even by force.

One example that many women might understand better is when a woman decides to buy a kilogram of tomatoes, and the price is 40 EGP. She then asks about the price for 10 kilograms and finds it costs only 350 EGP, so she decides to buy the 10 kilograms to save money. But when she returns, she might need to pay extra for the heavy load. More importantly, she will need to store the tomatoes in the fridge, which increases electricity usage beyond the 50 EGP she saved.

This is why we always conduct feasibility studies before major projects. The price difference between tomatoes and electricity may be small, but in business, the production cost may be many times more than the purchase or import cost. Except for strategic goods, no one wants to spend 50 EGP for every remote control compared to the 20 EGP import cost.

So, these detailed feasibility studies may not always help us reduce the lost value, but at least they give us a broader perspective on those lost values in construction and production.

Ignoring the Validity of Value

No matter what we're evaluating, it has a shelf life, after which it either loses its value completely or partially. Even the information you study can be forgotten over time. Perhaps after a year or two, when you sit for an exam in your final year of school, you won't be able to solve the problems you once analyzed.

What if you decide to travel to a country, and this trip requires a language test, and you find a discount for the test? But you won't be traveling for another two years. In this case, the test will no longer have value after two years. So, if you think that a 20% discount on the price is beneficial, the complete loss of the test's value will be of no use.

Some things have a validity period of years, like metals, while others are valid only for days, like yogurt, fresh vegetables, and fruits. A trader may buy vegetables at price "S" and later sell them for 2S, and after two days, the price may drop to S, and after four days, to half of S, and perhaps after a week, they give it away for free to dispose of it because it no longer has value for you but is useful for someone else, such as for use as organic fertilizer.

The validity of value is not just in non-consumable goods, such as food; sometimes, it's in fashion. For example, the price of a certain clothing model may be high when initially priced in the market, but after two years, it becomes undesirable, reducing its price. Similarly, the value of certain items differs depending on the location. Perhaps a certain amount of alcohol has value in one country, but once you cross borders to another, it becomes a problem, as its value is negative because it is not allowed in that country.

The value of a kilogram of gold might be very useful, but if you are on a sinking ship or a crashing plane, or inside a collapsed tunnel, it would be worth nothing—just a sip of water would be more valuable.

This is why in our lives, we might spend years searching for gold and money, but forget to secure the sip of water when the tunnel collapses, the plane crashes, or the ship sinks. Similarly, money in the bank might earn a little interest annually, but you need cash in hand for transportation or to buy food at a simple restaurant. The value of your assets when you can control them is not the same as their value when some country enforces sanctions on your money.

Simply put, we need to consider the validity of what we own—whether we can truly use it. Some say, "Don't put all your eggs in one basket," while others say, "Focus your efforts." But the most important thing is to understand these concepts, and then you will easily decide which one is worthwhile in each situation.

Poor Storage of Value

One of the causes of failure is storing the value you possess in a way that does not preserve its value. Yes, simply because value is not an absolute form. A block of ice might be worth 20 EGP, but after two hours in the open air, it might be worth nothing—or even negative in value because of the moisture it leaves behind in the area where it was stored.

The situation with ice is clear, but in other matters, it might be hidden enough that some people ignore it. For example, storing money in banks may seem safer, but over time, with rising inflation, the money will lose its value because its numerical value remains constant, while its purchasing power diminishes.

It's not just about money. If you acquire a language learning course but only keep the certificate and forget to refresh your language skills, this is poor storage. It's one of the causes of failure because your brain will eventually discard the information as a way of lightening the load. You may have learned the skill, but your mind, or let's say your brain, doesn't see you using it, and so it thinks, "Why should we keep storing this information if it's not being used?"

It's like buying a car and waiting until it appreciates in value, then selling it while leaving it on the street. Aside from the cost of storage, you are also storing it in a way that decreases its value.

This can also apply to an institution that decides to build housing in the desert, waiting for its price to rise before selling it or delaying delivery to raise the unit price. This is also an example of poor storage.

I lived in an apartment in Osman's housing complex in 6th October, Egypt, while I worked in the steel reinforcement field in nearby housing projects. I heard many stories about the looting of these buildings and the stealing of doors, electrical wires, and even staircase marble. This is simply because it's poor storage of value—the apartment is empty, and no one is guarding it.

This forms part of the lost values due to poor storage or storing for too long. An ice block might need a day in a low-temperature environment to change from water to ice, but it will require additional cooling energy for every day it stays frozen without returning to water.

Another issue with poor storage of goods and values is that it might lead to failure due to environmental changes. For instance, some countries maintain low production of gas fields to raise its market price while preserving their wells and reserves. But demand changes as countries shift toward safer nuclear energy.

In some cases, storing gas and oil might also be poor storage because it's outside their land. For example, some gas and oil wells cross countries' borders. Therefore, by reducing production in one country, the value of the gas and oil doesn't stay within that country because neighboring countries can extract it.

Another example of value ignorance is forgotten storage, such as buying a book, putting it on a shelf, and then transferring it to a desk drawer. This is poor storage because no reading schedule is planned for it.

Rising Inflation Rates

Some may view inflation as one of the environmental causes of failure, believing it cannot be controlled. However, in reality, it is one of the causes that people can avoid.

You don't need to view inflation as a problem as long as you don't store money.

I know you may store money as a company, perhaps for employees' salaries or even for emergencies. However, as long as this value is at a minimum and is set aside to address a single problem—not all problems—you might opt to make the market value of the company tangible by transforming it into actual products instead of just holding money in the stock market. Thus, this small amount you keep for a short time often doesn't exceed two percent.

Here, inflation doesn't affect the products you own, but only the money.

If you own manufacturing equipment or even products, inflation won't affect you. The key is to avoid poor storage.

Even if you keep financial values for some reason, real currencies (gold and silver) are always a better option. Paper currencies are simply fluctuating values that decrease because every morning the quantity of paper money increases, but the quantity of products does not. Therefore, people who hold paper money are increasing, while possessions remain the same. On the other hand, gold extraction aligns with global product growth.

As long as you stay away from storing money, let the money change. But if, for example, you keep the purchase price of a specific machine and store it for a month or a year, after a year, you won't be able to buy it.

But if you own real currencies, the price may decrease relatively compared to those currencies since the product became more available.

Temporal Value

Perhaps all values change, even if slightly, in proportion to each other. But some values are known to be temporal values.

For example, during the COVID-19 era, the value of face masks was much higher than now due to the increased need for them.

Simply put, value changes according to the need for it. The original evaluation is based on your need for it, not its market evaluation.

For instance, the value of gold is high, but if a ship is sinking, which is more important: the gold or the boats for survival?

Perhaps the value of a compass inside your phone is more useful than a mechanical compass outside it.

Because you don't need to carry extra weight in your pocket each morning, but if you lose your way in the desert, the external compass becomes more valuable, while your phone might have run out of charge.

Perhaps a cup of water near a river is of little value, but in a dry and hot place, it will be extremely valuable and costly.

One reason for failure is that we view value as absolute and forget its determinants. For example, it might be difficult for a factory to manufacture a sewing needle for 20 pounds, while it could import it for 5 pounds.

But strangely, in some cases, manufacturing certain products is better. For instance, weapons manufacturing cannot be evaluated in terms of the cheapest option but the most sustainable one. During a war, the same countries that offer you cheap or even free weapons as aid may stop supplying you.

This might seem strange on the surface, but in depth, it's not.

Temporal value is determined by a formula that considers our need for it and subtracts the times when it might stop being useful.

For example, buying expensive food from a friendly country or even locally is worth more than buying the same food from an enemy country. The time lost during a conflict or the reduced access to the food diminishes its value.

Incorrect Value Estimation

This incorrect estimation arises from all the reasons mentioned earlier, leading to an inaccurate evaluation of something—whether overestimated or underestimated. For example, you might value one shoe higher than another or consider a course you're about to take more important than it actually is.

Why does incorrect estimation cause failure?

Simply because you won't know which things are more valuable than others. For example, in medical practice, safety procedures for an injured person prioritize checking blood circulation, respiration, and airways.

But what about a patient with weak breathing who is bleeding from a finger?

Protocols may vary on whether airway management or circulation is more important. The truth is, a finger bleed is usually less of an emergency than breathing problems, as the bleed tends to stop on its own. However, the situation may dictate that respiratory issues are more critical.

What we've done is just hypothesize, but the actual value of this bleeding as a danger and priority is incorrectly assessed because we don't directly see the bleeding.

The basic principle is that value estimation should come after seeing the situation first-hand.

As some say, don't buy fish in water—not just because you don't know if it will be caught but because you don't know how it will be caught and how much value is lost in the process.

For instance, a butcher may decide to buy livestock over the phone, agreeing on the price per kilogram. However, upon reaching the location, he might be surprised by the long road that requires additional transport costs. This will affect the overall value because the transport cost must be factored in.

Correct estimation often gets overlooked, whether dealing with personal or institutional matters. However, the most important point is that any estimation process may not be 100% accurate, and we only approximate as closely as possible.

The second point is that value estimation on paper is usually better, and the more experience you have, the more accurate your estimates become as long as you continue to write, learn, and benefit from your experiences.

Mathematical Calculation of Value

It might seem strange when we say one plus one doesn't equal two.

We all learned basic math in school, but in practice, this can be true. Even chemists know that one liter of water and one liter of alcohol will not equal two liters of a water-alcohol mixture but less.

It sounds strange, but it's the reality.

In practical life, many things can't be calculated arithmetically, and doing so might lead to disastrous consequences.

Simply because some things are valued depending on circumstances and demand.

For example, if the price of one kilogram of rice is 30 pounds, it might be easy to say that five kilograms will cost 150 pounds.

But some might be more clever and estimate the price to be slightly lower, perhaps 145 pounds.

Here, you are not making a simple mathematical estimation of value.

This could affect the accuracy of many plans, but it's usually expected.

Now imagine saying that one million tons or one billion tons of rice would cost 30 million or 30 billion pounds.

It would not be less, simply because when you buy five kilograms, you reduce the number of weighing times, and the cost may drop since fewer bags are required. But when you buy a million or a billion tons, the dynamics of demand change, and people will need the rice and be willing to pay more. This will drive the price up, maybe even doubling it as supply decreases.

The equation may not be precise, but the fact remains that the more the demand exceeds supply, the higher the price will go.

This might sound absurd, but it applies to labor as well.

If you manage a small factory in a village and think the wage of a worker is 200 pounds per day, when you need half the village's population to work, you may find that not all will want to work with you, preferring to work elsewhere. This will force you to increase wages to attract workers.

Unaccounted Values

Whether in our personal lives or professional business, there are many unaccounted values that are often emotional and relational, which cannot be measured in monetary terms but are of great value.

For example, an employee at a company might risk his life to save the company. This might seem foolish, but it may be because the manager once said to him, "Even if we don’t need what you're doing, we still need you."

This may seem dramatic, but every day, thousands of unaccounted values exist: loyalty from employees, friends, and respect from people.

There are many things we can’t claim ownership of because they are not for sale, but they provide protection, kindness, and good manners.

Doesn’t this matter?

Yes, it does. It’s part of calculating other values.

Customer trust increases the likelihood of repeat purchases and, over time, turns marketing from an active process to a passive one that happens through the company’s reputation and customer satisfaction.

Or even if an employee recommends you for a new job, you can't sell the value of your knowledge to that person, but it will benefit you.

Whether for an individual or an organization, these are things outside of mathematical and non-mathematical calculations. They are often felt, not rationalized.

For instance, an employee may reject a higher-paying offer simply to avoid leaving his job because of the good treatment he receives, even though his working hours have ended.

Sometimes, people might view me as less emotional, and this might be true.

However, what's strange is that even those unaccounted values have priorities and proportions.

They follow the law of fixed quantity, meaning the more you take, the less you have.

Therefore, you must distribute those unaccounted values according to need and preset assumptions.

Perhaps your wife needs more affection than your work colleague, even though affection is required by both. Your children may need more affection than your clients, even though your clients might require better treatment.

You may need the loyalty of your employees or clients, but some employees or clients will need it more than others.

This is where the wisdom of distributing these unaccounted values comes into play, including affection, smiles, and laughter

Also by Ahmed Ragab Ali Abdelghany

Nursing AI war
Artificial intelligence managed Hospitals
Abc of ABC
مبادئ السيطرة في الفكر المعاصر
٩٧ سببا للفشل
Principles of Mind Control
97 Causes for Failure

Also by Msytr

Nursing AI war
Artificial intelligence managed Hospitals
Abc of ABC
٩٧ سببا للفشل
Principles of Mind Control
97 Causes for Failure

www.ingramcontent.com/pod-product-compliance
Lightning Source LLC
LaVergne TN
LVHW050546160826
845677LV00011B/2198

9798230538561